中华传统经典养生术

（汉英对照）

(Chinese-English) Traditional and Classical Chinese Health Cultivation

| | |
|---|---|
| Chief Producer Li Jie | 总策划 李 洁 |
| Chief Compilers Li Jie Xu Feng Xiao Bin Zhao Xiaoting | 总主编 李 洁 许 蜂 肖 斌 赵晓霆 |
| Chief Translator Han Chouping | 总主译 韩丑萍 |
| English Language Reviewer Lawrence Lau | 英译主审 劳伦斯·刘 |

# 八段锦

*Ba Duan Jin*

编著 赵晓霆
Compiler Zhao Xiaoting

翻译 韩丑萍
Translator Han Chouping

上海科学技术出版社
Shanghai Scientific & Technical Publishers

I0110546

图书在版编目（CIP）数据

八段锦：汉英对照 / 赵晓霆编著；韩丑萍译.—
上海：上海科学技术出版社，2015.5
（中华传统经典养生术）
ISBN 978-7-5478-2552-5

Ⅰ.①八… Ⅱ.①赵… ②韩… Ⅲ.①八段锦–基本
知识–汉、英 Ⅳ.①G852.9

中国版本图书馆CIP数据核字（2015）第042361号

**八段锦**

编著 赵晓霆

上海世纪出版股份有限公司
上海科学技术出版社 出版

中国图书进出口上海公司 发行

2015年5月第1版
ISBN 978-7-5478-2552-5/R · 874

# 顾问委员会

# 编纂委员会

**总策划**

李　洁

Chief Producer

Li Jie

**总主编**

李　洁　许　峰　肖　斌　赵晓霆

Chief Compilers

Li Jie　Xu Feng　Xiao Bin　Zhao Xiaoting

**副总主编**

孙　磊　陈昌乐　倪青根

Vice Chief Compilers

Sun Lei　Chen Changle　Ni Qinggen

**总主译**

韩丑萍

Chief Translator

Han Chouping

**副主译**

赵海磊

Vice Chief Translator

Zhao Hailei

# 项目资助

Acknowledgement

· 上海市新闻出版专项扶持资金项目

· 上海市中医药三年行动计划（2015—2018年）"基于〈中华气功史陈列馆〉科普教育基地为核心的〈中医气功文化平台〉建设"（项目编号：ZY3–WHJS–1–1010）

· Shanghai Press and Publication of special support funds program

· The Three-Year Action Plan for Chinese Medicine in Shanghai (2015–2018) on Construction of Qigong Cultural Platform in the Museum of Chinese Qigong History (Program No: ZY3–WHJS–1–1010)

# 序

欣闻上海市气功研究所编写的《中华传统经典养生术》丛书即将出版，这是中华原创医学文明传播的一件盛事，特致贺忱。

中华传统养生术源远流长，其中导引术更是重要的组成部分，它先于针、灸、药、医而形成，是中华民族最早用以防治疾病、养生保健的重要方法之一。现存早期文献《庄子》《吕氏春秋》《黄帝内经》以及考古发现《引书》《导引图》中均有关于养生导引及其具体方法的记载。此后绵绵数千年的历史长河中，中华养生导引术不断丰富、发展与创新，在自我实践中形成千门万法，在去伪存真中完善理论体系。20世纪后叶，古之导引术又以现代"气功"的面目再次席卷中华大地，并享誉海内外。时至今天，中华导引术仍然以其"人天合一"的整体观思想与丰富多姿的养生导引方法独立于世界自然医药之林，滋润着人类身心世界。事实表明，中华导引术已经形成为一门博大精深的学术体系。它所研究的是人之物质基础（精）与自组织能力（神）相互关系的规律，是关于"人"——这个地球上最复杂系统达到和谐与协调的一门学问。

我和上海市气功研究所相识逾30年，该所自20世纪70年代的中医研究所开始，气功与导引就是关注、研究的重点领域；80年代中期更名气功研究所后，更是全力着眼于现代气功的研究与中华导引术的弘扬。《中华传统经典养生术》是上海市气功研究所多年来所教授养生导引术、气功功法的汇编与总结，对于帮助学习、普及推广现代导引术具有较好的价值。希望此丛书的出版，能够进一步带动当前养生导引术在海内外的健康发展，推动中华优秀文化走向世界各地。

是以为序。

林中鹏

2015年3月

It is with great pleasure that I learn the *Traditional and Classical Chinese Health Cultivation* series compiled by the Shanghai Qigong Research Institute will be published soon. This means a lot to the spread of Chinese medical civilization.

Traditional Chinese health cultivation has a long-standing and well-established history. As an important part of health cultivation practice, Dao Yin exercise was used for disease prevention and treatment as well as life cultivation before acupuncture, moxibustion and herbal medicine. The recordings of *Dao Yin* and its specific exercise methods can be traced back to the *Zhuangzi, Lü Shi Chun Qiu* (The Annals of Lü Buwei), *Huang Di Nei Jing* (the Yellow Emperor's Inner Classic) and archaeologically unearthed books such as *Yin Shu* (a book on Dao Yin) and *Dao Yin Tu* (Dao Yin Diagram). After this, the thousands of years have witnessed the enrichment, progress and innovation of Chinese *Dao Yin* practice, coupled with emergence of numerous methods and perfection of its theoretical system. In late 20th century, the ancient *Dao Yin* exercise became exceptionally popular across China in the form of 'qigong'. Today, Chinese *Dao Yin* exercise remains flourish with its holistic 'Man-Nature Unity' idea and various exercise methods that benefit both body and mind. Facts show that there is a profound academic system behind Chinese *Dao Yin* exercise. This system studies the interactions between material foundation (essence) and self-organization ability (mind). In other words, it studies the way to achieve harmony and coordination of human being—the most complex system on earth.

I've established a friendship with the Shanghai Qigong Research Institute for 30 years. Ever since its founding in 1970s as a Research Institute of Chinese Medicine, qigong and *Dao Yin* have always been the research priorities of the Institute. The focuses on qigong and *Dao Yin* have been more highlighted in 1980s when the Institute was renamed as a Qigong Research Institute. I firmly believe that the

*Traditional and Classical Chinese Health Cultivation* series are of great significance in popularizing modern *Dao Yin* exercise. I sincerely wish the book series can further promote *Dao Yin* exercise at home and abroad and spread excellent Chinese culture.

For this, I wrote this forward.

Lin Zhongpeng
March  2015

# 前　言

## 气 以 臻 道

农历乙未早春,正是上海市气功研究所创建三十周年之际,恰逢气功学术发展枯木迎春之季。在此,我们谨向海内外气功学界发出倡言——构建现代气功"气以臻道"的学术思想。

所谓"气以臻道",首先是指气功学术发展必须树立一个大方向,即中华传统文化精神的最高目标——"道";其次是指通过对"气"的感性体验与理性认知,使生命更趋向"道",与"道"合一。道者,规律、目标也;气者,方法、途径;臻者,趋向、完善也。气-道共同构成"气以臻道"学术思想内核。其中气为实、主行,是具体之指;道为虚、主理,是抽象之喻。气因道而展,道由气而实;气以道归,道以气显;气借道而实际指归,道假气而理性论证。气功学术发展必须气、道并重,互印互证,理行一贯。两者既各尽其责、各擅其能,又有主从之别。"道"因标指形上本体而为万法归宗之源;"气"每描述形下万法而成法法生灭之流。"道"经思维抽象提炼,揭示规律、规则之理性思辨;"气"常直叙主观感觉,表述体会、觉受的感性认识。道-气,一主一从,一虚一实,构成中华气功学术思想的本质内涵。

"气以臻道"学术思想之主体是"道",是指向真理之道路,是学术文化人文精神的体现,也是先人用身心去实践生命运化规律的心得体验,古人称为"内证之学"。"道"的外延旁及"功"和"术",可以包括各种神秘现象、气功现象、特异现象,古人称为"神通法术"。当今,现代科学研究介入传统气功学术是时代进步的表现,它为我们观察生命奥秘打开了一个全新的视角。透过唯象的研究,重新激发起人类对生命的思考与敬重,重新挖掘出科技文明下的人文精神,而非单纯地将生命物质化,这才是现代科学介入传统气功的人文价值所在。

有鉴于此,我们倡议构建现代气功研究之"气以臻道"学术思想,让中华传统文化与现代科学携起手来,揭示生命真谛,回归大道本源。

上海市气功研究所

2015年春

## Advocacy for *Qi-Dao Harmony* in Modern Qigong Practice

The year 2015 is a Chinese new year of yin wood sheep (*Yi Wei* in Chinese). Wood, in Chinese culture on five elements (*Wu Xing*), is connected to the season of spring. The year 2015 also marks the 30th anniversary of the founding of Shanghai Qigong Research Institute. With a strong belief that the spring of 2015 will bring new hope to qigong study, we hereby advocate the concept of 'Qi-*Dao Harmony*' for its academic advance.

The term *Qi-Dao Harmony* has two underlying implications. First, it implies that *dao* is the ultimate goal of traditional Chinese culture and the general orientation for academic qigong advance. Second, it implies that our lives shall combine into one with the *dao* through perception and understanding of qi. In summary, this term means to achieve and perfect *dao* through qi exercise. The 'qi' here is weighted and refers to practice. The '*dao*' here is unweighted and refers to principles. Without *dao*, qi cannot extend; without qi, *dao* cannot become weighted. Qi finds its origin in *dao* and *dao* manifests itself in qi. Qi returns to *dao* eventually and *dao* supports qi theoretically. It's essential for people in academic qigong field to pay equal attention to qi and *dao*. The two have a principal-subordinate relationship. The metaphysical *dao* is the origin of all methods. The physical qi is the practice of all methods. *Dao* is about the abstract thinking and reveals the laws and rules. Qi is about the subjective feelings and tells experience and perception. Qi and *dao* constitute the essence of academic idea in Chinese qigong.

Let's get a deeper look into the concept of *Qi-Dao Harmony*. Also known as the 'learning of internal evidence', *dao* is the way to truth. It contains humanistic spirit and physical and mental experience of our ancestors. *Dao* extends to exercise (*gong*) and a variety of magic arts including mysterious, qigong and extrasensory phenomena. Today, modern scientific qigong research offers a new insight into the mysteries of life. The phenomenological research rekindles our reflection and respect towards life and enables us to re-discover humanism from modern civilization greatly impacted by science and technology. This is the real value of scientific research on traditional qigong in this materialized world.

To this end, we advocate the academic concept of '*Qi-Dao Harmony*' in modern qigong research. We believe the combination of traditional Chinese culture and modern science can help us to reveal the truth of life and return to the origin of the great *dao*.

Shanghai Qigong Research Institute

Spring  2015

# 编写说明

Words from the Compilers

中华传统养生术根植于中国传统哲学、中医学和养生学，是人体自我身心锻炼的有效方法。

随着倡导"主动健康"概念日益深入人心，具有调身、调息、调心功能的中华传统养生术，以其传统的养修理论、独特的身心效果蜚声海内外，引起世人的广泛关注。但近期国内外少见中国传统养生术的书籍出版，尤其没有成套、成系列的经典养生类作品问世，更缺乏英汉对照的专业著作。

上海中医药大学上海市气功研究所研究人员在前期研究工作基础上，精选中华传统经典养生术共八种，从历史源流、功法理论、特色要领、图解动作、分解说明与具体运用几方面进行中文编纂，由上海中医药大学中医英语专业人员进行翻译。并邀请专家进行中文审稿，邀请美国友三中医药大学Lawrence Lau先生审定英文翻译。

本套丛书详细地将八种中华经典养生术以图文并茂、视频摄像的形式记录下来，配以光盘，非常方便学习与传播，尤其便于海外养生爱好者以英语来学习。

本套丛书编纂过程中，得到上海市中医药三年行动计划（2015—2018年）"基于〈中华气功史陈列馆〉科普教育基地为核心的〈中医气功文化平台〉建设"（项目编号：ZY3-WHJS-1-1010）资助。

编者

Traditional Chinese health cultivation includes a variety of body-mind exercises, which are deeply rooted in ancient Chinese philosophy and medicine.

Today, the concept of 'health initiative (an ability to achieve physical, mental and social well-being)' has become well recognized.

Traditional Chinese health cultivation exercises are attracting worldwide attention because of their unique effects in regulating the breathing, body and mind. However, there are few books in this regard, especially the classical book series. There are even fewer bilingual Chinese-English versions of these books.

Based on their previous studies, research staff at the Shanghai Qigong Research Institute compiled eight traditional and classical health cultivation exercise methods, covering their history, theoretical foundation, characteristics and key principles, illustrated movements and application. Then these contents have been translated by professional interpreters at Shanghai University of Traditional Chinese Medicine. The Chinese version was reviewed by an expert team. The English version was reviewed by Dr. Lawrence Lau at the Yo San University of Traditional Chinese Medicine.

In addition to illustrations and videos are also available for readers, especially overseas health cultivation fans to learn.

This books series have been funded by the Three-Year Action Plan for Chinese Medicine in Shanghai (2015–2018) on Construction of Qigong Cultural Platform in the Museum of Chinese Qigong History (Program No: ZY3–WHJS–1–1010).

Compilers

# 目 录

Table of Contents

History

源流

八段锦是一个有千年历史的经典功法，一般由八个主要动作组成，"锦"指此套功法珍贵、优秀。相传道家神仙用以筑基培元；释家高僧辅以参禅修定；民间多以强身健体，祛病延年。

*Ba Duan Jin* is an ancient practice that can be traced back to thousands of years ago. It consists of eight movements. Literally, the word *Jin* means precious or valuable (a silken quality like a piece of brocade). According to legend, Daoist immortals practiced *Ba Duan Jin* to lay foundations for inner alchemy and eminent monks practiced *Ba Duan Jin* for *Chan (Zen)*-meditation. The common people practiced Ba Duan Jin to remove diseases and improve health.

八段锦的起源以及演变是个非常漫长的过程。

*Ba Duan Jin* has a very long history of development.

据传，东晋道士许逊，豫章南昌人，净明道派尊奉的祖师，就是"一人得道，鸡犬升天"中所说的神功妙济真君许逊，相传著有《灵剑子》等道教经典。

As the story goes, a Daoist priest in the East Jin dynasty (317–420) named Xu Xun (from Yuzhang, Nanchang, Jiangxi Province) was the patriarch of Jing Ming Daoist Branch (Pure Brightness Sect). He was also the legendary Sublime Saviour of Divine Virtuosity (*Shen Gong Miao Ji Zhen Jun*) of "when a man attains the Dao, all his family including fowls and dogs ascend to the heaven". In addition, Xu Xun was also the author of Daoism classics including *Ling Jian Zi*.

《灵剑子引导子午记·引导诀》云："仰托一度理三焦,左肝右肺如射雕,东肝单托西通肾,五劳回顾七伤调。游鱼摆尾通心脏,手攀双足理于腰,次鸣天鼓三十六,两手掩耳后头敲。"(《道藏》第十册)八句概括了七个动作,此口诀虽无八段锦之名,实为后世八段锦早期的歌诀形式。许真君曾自言遇上天真圣传授"太上灵宝净明法",有斩蛟擒妖道法。传说他曾斩蛟龙,为民除害,道法高妙,声闻遐迩,活到136岁,于东晋宁康二年(374年)八月初一日合家四十二人连同鸡犬一齐飞天成仙,世人尊奉他为"许仙"。飞升前,许逊将宝剑插在宅宇的屋脊上,一是为了防止螭吻(龙之第九子)离去(使其永远喷水镇火),二是为了镇慑妖邪。至今,江西许姓视许逊为保护神。

The *Ling Jian Zi Yin Dao Zi Wu Ji Yin Dao Jue* (Ling Jian-zi's Record of *Dao Yin* between the Hours of Zi and Wu) states, "Two hands hold up the heaven to regulate *Sanjiao*, drawing the bow left (the liver) and right (the lung) to shoot the hawk, strengthen the liver and kidneys using two hands, hold the left elbow with the right hand and look to the left and vice versa to regulate emotions, abduce and shake two arms to benefit the heart, two hands hold the soles to strengthen the low back, and cover the ears with two hands to click teeth 36 times, and tap the postauricular bone using the index finger" (the volume 10 of the *Daozang* or *Daoist Canon*). These eight sentences summarized seven movements. Although these movements were not named as Ba Duan Jin, they are the early verses of Ba Duan Jin.

According to Xu Xun, he once learned the *Tai Shang Ling Bao Jing Ming Fa* from an immortal, including the method of fighting against dragons and killing of snakes. During his official service, he had done many things to help the people.

Xu Xun was already 136 years old in the second year of Ningkang (374). On the first day of the eighth lunar month of that year, his whole family of 42 persons ascended to the heaven, together with their fowls and dogs. He was venerated as Xu Immortal (*Xian*). Before ascending to the heaven, Xu Xun thrust his sword into the roof of his house. This had two purposes: one is to keep the ninth son of the dragon spraying water to suppress fire; the other is to repel demons and evil spirits. Today, Xu families in Jiangxi province still consider Xu Xun as their guarding angel.

---

南朝梁代陶弘景（456—536年），字通明，南朝梁时丹阳秣陵（今江苏南京）人，号华阳隐居。著名的医药家、炼丹家、文学家，人称"山中宰相"。梁武帝曾经下诏问陶弘景"山中何所有"？言下之意是说山中什么也没有，还不如出来做官，也就什么都有了。陶弘景写了"诏问山中何所有赋诗以答"："山中何所有？岭上多白云。只可自怡悦，不堪持赠君。"山中有什么？岭上有许多怡然自得的白云，可惜我赏悦，却难以用手捧来送给您啊！巧妙地表示了自己不愿出山做官，不屑与时人为伍的高雅志向。他对阐扬道教，尤付精力，继承《上清》经法，开创茅山宗，是南朝道教中最有影响的人物，对后世道教的发展影响亦较深远。撰有《养性延命录》，此书总结了魏晋以前的养生理论和方法，书中所描述的左右挽弓势、左右单托天势、两手前筑势，与清末定型的八段锦中"五劳七伤往后瞧""背后七颠百病消""左右开弓似射雕""调整理脾胃须单举""攒拳怒目增气力"五种动作相仿。

Tao Hongjing (456–536), style name (or courtesy name) Tongming and pseudonym Hua Yang Yin Ju (*Hua Yang recluse*), lived in the Southern Liang dynasty (502–557). Born in Moling, Danyang (now Nanjing, Jiangsu Province), Tao Hongjing was a well-known medical expert, alchemist and writer. Although he lived a secluded life in the mountains, he remained an adviser and friend to the then emperor Wu of Liang. Consequently, Tao Hongjing had the nickname *Prime Minister in the Mountains*. The emperor Wu of Liang once issued an imperial edict saying 'what can the mountains offer you"? (Implying that there's nothing in the mountains and he should be a government official). Tao Hongjing wrote a poem to reply the emperor:

What can the mountains offer me?

Nothing but the clouds white and free.

Though enjoy the scene with content,

To you, my lord, I'm shy to present.

After declining the emperor's invitation, Tao Hongjing devoted himself to in-depth study of Daoism. He further developed the Supreme Clarity (Shang Qing Dao) and became the real founder of Mao Shan (Mt. Mao) Sect. He has been considered as an eminent and influential Daoist figure in the Southern dynasty (420–589). His book *Records on Nourishing Character & Prolonging Life* (*Yang Xing Yan Ming Lu*) summarized the principles and practice on nurturing life before the Wei and Jin period (220–420). Some movements recorded in this book (e.g., drawing a blow to left and right, hold up the heaven using alternate hands and two hands hold the feet, etc.) are very similar to Ba Duan Jin movements (e.g., look back to alleviate overstrain and emotions, bouncing (7 times) on the feet, toes, heel, drawing the bow to shoot the hawk, raise hand on each side to adjust the spleen & stomach and clench the fists and glare fiercely to increase general vitality and muscular strength, etc.) in the late Qing dynasty (1644–1912).

八段锦之名，最早见于北宋洪迈《夷坚志》，并称为"长生安乐法"，但未记载八段锦的具体功法。南宋绍兴二十一年（1151

年)刊行的晁公武《郡斋读书志》,载有"《八段锦》一卷,不题撰人,吐故纳新之诀也",但原书已佚。陆游《清尊录》曾提到北宋镇边大将军姚平仲出道后在庐山向他人传授八段锦。

The term of Ba Duan Jin was first recorded as *Longevity and Wellness Exercise* (*Chang Sheng An Le Fa*) in the *Yi Jian Zhi* by Hong Mai in the Song Dynasty (960–1279); however, there were no detailed movements in the book. The *Jun Zhai Du Shu Zhi* compiled by Chao Gongwu in 1151 states, "Ba Duan Jin (whose author is unknown) is about rhymes of breathing out the stale and breathing in the fresh". Unfortunately this book was lost. Lu You[1] mentioned in the *Qing Zun Lu* that General Yao Pingzhong in Northern Song Dynasty (960–1127) had taught Ba Duan Jin in Mount Lu.

南宋初年著名道教学者曾慥(字端伯,号至游居士、至游子)在汇集宋以前文献的《修真十书·杂著捷径》卷二十三《临江仙》词附注中有记载,原文谓:"钟离先生八段锦,吕公手书石壁上,因传于世。其后又有窦银青八段锦,与小崔先生临江仙词,添六字气其中,恨其词未尽,予因择诸家之善,作临江仙一阕,简而备,且易行。普劝遵修,同证道果。绍兴辛未(1151年)仲春,至游居士曾慥记。"据此可知,宋时八段锦有四家,窦银青和小崔先生二家今已佚。曾慥在小崔先生八段锦基础上加六字气诀,并以词加注的形式创编了曾慥八段锦。钟离,指唐代钟离权(字云房),亦称汉钟离,传说八仙之一,其内丹术传吕洞宾。《修真十书·杂著捷径》卷十九载有钟离八段锦法。现将两家八段锦原文引录于下。

Zeng Zao (courtesy name *Duan Bo*, pseudonym *Zhi You Ju Shi* or *Zhi You Zi*), an eminent Daoist scholar in early years of the Southern Song Dynasty recorded Ba Duan Jin in annotations

1. Lu You: a prominent poet of China's Southern Song Dynasty (1127—1279).

of the 23$^{rd}$ volume (*Lin Jiang Xian*, literally means Immortals on the River) of the *Xiu Zhen Shi Shu Za Zhu Jie Jing* (Shortcut to Miscellaneous Writings, Ten Books on Cultivating Perfection). According to the original text, Lü Dongbin[1] carved the Ba Duan Jin of Zhongli Quan[2] on the stone wall to pass down through generations. Thereafter, Ba Duan Jin of Dou Yinqing and Mr. Cui had been supplemented (unfortunately, these two versions were lost). Zeng Zao supplemented six-word healing sounds. The verses and interpretations of Zeng Zao Ba Duan Jin and Zhongli Ba Duan Jin are as follows:

## 曾慥八段锦

子后寅前东向坐,冥心琢齿(三十六)鸣鼉(鸣天鼓三十通),托天(三次,每次行嘻字气)回顾(握固按腿,左右各三,先右次左,左行嘘字气,右行㖠字气也)眼光摩(挫挪手,摩眼七次,闭目转睛七次,以中指节捻太阳三十六),张弓(左右二三十挽,每次行呵字气)仍踏弩(左右各三次,每次三挽七踏,行呵字气),升降辘轳多(左右运转辘轳三十六,行吹字气)。

**Zeng Zao *Ba Duan Jin*** (Volume 23, *Xiu Zhen Shi Shu Za Zhu Jie Jing*, Photocopy of Daozang, the Cultural Relics Publishing House, 1988):

Time: 11pm–1am; 3am–4am.

Sit down with a concentrated mind. Click the teeth (36 times) and hear the heavenly drum (36 times). Lift the arms up (3 times coupled with the healing sound of 'Xi'). Then flex the thumb under the other four fingers to press the thigh (3 times

---

1. Lü Dongbin: One of the earliest masters of Neidan or internal alchemy, a Tang Dynasty scholar and poet who has been elevated to the status of an Immortal in the Chinese cultural sphere.
2. Zhongli Quan: Courtesy name Yun Fang, one of the most ancient of the Eight Immortals and the leader of the group. He is also known as Zhongli of Han because he was said to be born during the Han Dynasty.

on each side (right thigh first), coupled with the healing sound of 'Xu' for left side and the healing sound of 'Dao'). Twist the hands and rub the eyes (7 times, close the eyes and turn the eyeballs 7 times, and twist Taiyang, an extra acupuncture point (36 times using the knuckle of the middle finger), draw a bow (20 or 30 times on each side coupled with the healing sound of 'he') and step the crossbow (3 times on each side, 3 times of drawing the bow and 7 times of stepping the crossbow, coupled with the healing sound of 'he'), and rotate the body like a pulley (rotate the body 36 times on each side coupled with the healing sound of 'chui').

三度朝元（三次，每次按腿、闭目、咽气，名为朝元。每次行吹字）九度转（想气自丹田转九交），背摩（盘足，闭气，搓手热，摩擦肾俞上下，行吹字气）双摆（按腿，冥目闭气，左右摇摆身，不限数，名鳌鱼摆尾，行呵字气）扳（舒脚，以手低头扳脚，行呵字气）拿（跪膝反手，左右拿脚跟三次，每次行呼字气），龙虎交际咽元和（以舌搅取津满口，漱三十六，一气分三回，想至丹田中，如此三遍，行吹字气），浴身（鼻引清气，闭住，搓按两手极热，遍身擦令微汗出）挑甲罢（左右臂举手齐发，遍挑十指甲，不限数），便可蹑烟萝（凡行吹肾、呵心、嘘肝、嘻三焦、呬肺、呼脾六字，不可令耳闻声，出气欲细而长。凡行持皆闭气，行持罢，方吐气出，呼所行字）。

（《道藏》，文物出版社等，1988年影印本第四册《修真十书·杂著捷径》卷二十三《临江仙》）

Conduct 3 times of *Chao Yuan*[1] (pressing the legs, closing the eyes and swallowing qi coupled with the healing sound of 'chui'), followed by 9 times of imagining that qi from the Dantian moving. After this, sit with crossed feet, hold the

---

1. A health cultivation practice in Daoism to gather qi of five-zang organs into the umbilicus (*Tian Yuan* in Chinese).

breath, twist the hands until they become warm and rub the surrounding area of Shenshu (BL 23)[1], coupled with the healing sound of 'chui'. Then press the legs, close the eyes, hold the breath and rotate the body to each side for a couple of times, coupled with the healing sound of 'he'. Pull the feet with the hands coupled with the healing sound of 'he' and grasp the heels (3 times for each foot) coupled with the healing sound of 'hu'. Touch the upper palate using the tongue to produce saliva, rinse the mouth 36 times with the saliva, swallow in three gulps and imagine descending the saliva to the Dantian. Repeat 3 times coupled with the healing sound of 'chui'. Breathe in through the nose, hold the breath, twist the hands until they become warm and then rub the body until presence of mild sweats. Raise left and right arms to ascend qi sensation to ten fingernails. Finally, pronounce the healing sounds of 'Chui' (for the kidney), 'He' (for the heart), 'Xu' (for the liver), 'Xi' (for Sanjiao), 'Dao' (for the lung) and 'Hu' (for the spleen) silently.

## 钟离八段锦

闭目冥心坐（冥心盘趺而坐），握固静思神。叩齿三十六，两手抑昆仑（叉两手向项后，数九息，勿令耳闻。自此以后，出入息皆不可使耳闻）。左右鸣天鼓，二十四度闻（移两手心掩两耳，先以第二指压中指，弹击脑后，左右各二十四次）。微摆撼天柱（摇头左右顾，肩膊随动二十四，先须握固），赤龙搅水浑（赤龙者，舌也，以舌搅口齿并左右颊，待津液生而咽）。漱津三十六（一云鼓漱），神水满口匀。一口分三咽（所漱津液分作三口作汩汩声而咽之），龙行虎自奔（液为龙，气为虎），闭气搓手热（以鼻引清气闭之，少项，搓手令热极，鼻中徐徐乃放气出），背摩后

---

1. Shenshu (BL 23): An acupuncture point located in the depression below the spinous process of L2, 1.5 cun lateral to the spine.

精门（精门者，腰后外肾也。合手心摩毕收手握固）。尽此一口气（再闭气也），想火烧脐轮（闭口鼻之气，想用心火下烧丹田，觉热极即用后法）。左右辘轳转（俯首摆撼两肩三十六，想火自丹田透双关，入脑户，鼻引清气，闭少顷间），两脚放舒伸（放直两脚）。叉手双虚托（叉手相交，向上托空三次或九次），低头攀脚频（以两手向前，攀脚心十二次，乃收足端坐），以候逆水上（候口中津液生，如未生，再用急搅取水，同前法），再漱再吞津。如此三度毕，神水九次吞（谓再漱三十六，如前一口分三咽，乃为九也）。咽下汩汩响，百脉自调匀。河车搬运讫（摆肩并身二十四次，再转辘轳二十四次），发火遍烧身（想丹田火自下而上，遍烧身体，想时口及鼻皆闭气少顷）。邪魔不敢近，梦寐不能昏。寒暑不能入，灾病不能箏。子后午前后，造化合乾坤。循环次第转，八卦是良因。

**Zhongli *Ba Duan Jin*** (Volume 19, *Xiu Zhen Shi Shu Za Zhu Jie Jing*):

Sit down with eyes closed and mind concentrated (concentrate the mind and sit with legs crossed). Flex the thumb under the other four fingers and click teeth 36 times. Cross the fingers, place them over the occiput and count 9 times of breaths silently (Do not make it audible. After that, keep the inhalation and exhalation inaudible).

Then, sound the left and right heavenly drums for 24 times (cover both ears with the centers of palms. First press the middle finger with the index finger and then tap the occiput 24 times on each side using the index finger).

Slightly sway to shake the heavenly pillar (Turn the head to the left and right, eyes looking backwards as far as possible. Move the shoulders and arms simultaneously. Repeat 24 times on each side. Be sure to flex the thumb under the other four fingers first).

The red dragon stirs the water (The red dragon here refers to the tongue. Touch the teeth, gum and upper palate using the tip of the tongue to produce saliva). Rinse the mouth with the saliva 36 times (also known as drum rinsing) until your mouth becomes filled with saliva, swallow it in three gulps with a gurgling sound. In this way, the dragon (fluid) and tiger (qi) will naturally run (circulate smoothly).

Hold the breath and rub the hands until they become warm (Take a deep breath through the nose and hold it for a while. Rub the hands until they become really warm. Then slowly breathe out). Then use the palms to rub the Jingmen on the back (Jingmen literally means essential gate, here refers to the kidney). Return and flex the thumb under the other four fingers. After this breath is exhausted (hold the breath again), imagine fire burning the Manipura (hold the breath in the mouth and nose and imagine sending heart fire down to burn the Dantian area until you feel extremely warm).

Rotate the body to the left and right like a pulley (lower the head and shake shoulders 36 times to each side. Imaging the fire from Dantian to ascend through the Jia Ji pass[1] and Yu Zhen Pass[2] and enter the brain. Take a deep breath through the nose and hold it for a while). Relax both legs (stretch both legs).

Cross hands and raise the palms up (cross both hands and push them up for 3 or 9 times).

Lower the head and touch the feet with both hands (Touch the soles using both hands 12 times. Then return the feet and sit upright). Wait for the water to ascend (Wait for the saliva to be produced in the mouth. If it does not appear, use the aforementioned method to produce saliva). Then rinse the

---

1. One the of the three passes, also known as the Lu Lu pass or double Jia Ji passes. Location: on the back and at the midpoint of the line connecting bilateral olecranon in a prone position.
2. One of the three passes in the occiput, Yu Zhen literally means the Jade Pillow. Location: slightly below the point Yuzhen (BL 9) and in between bilateral Fengchi (GB 20). It is the last pass along the Du meridian that the internal qi has to overcome.

mouth and swallow the saliva. Repeat this 3 times and swallow the divine water (saliva) 9 times (this means to rinse the mouth for 36 times more and then swallow it in three gulps as mentioned above). Swallow with a gurgling sound. This can harmonize all channels.

Along with a smooth circulation of qi and blood within the microcosmic and macrocosmic orbits, (sway the shoulders and the body 24 times coupled with 24 times of rotating the body like a pulley), start the fire to burn the entire body (imagine that Dantian fire burns the entire body from bottom to top. At the same time, hold the breath in the mouth and nose for a while). This will keep away evil spirits and pathogenic factors and result in good sleep. This exercise should be done after the period between 11 pm and 1 am and before the period between 11 pm and 1 am. It's advisable to follow the sequence of the eight movements and directions.

诀曰：“其法于甲子日，夜半子时起首，行时口中不得出气，唯鼻中微放清气。每日子后午前各行一次，或昼夜共行三次。久而自知，蠲除疾疫，渐觉身轻。若能勤苦不怠，则仙道不远矣。”

（《修真十书·杂著捷径》卷十九）

The verses states, '... during Ba Duan Jin exercise, breathe through the nose instead of the mouth. This exercise can be practiced two or three times a day. Over time, this can help remove chronic conditions and promote health. Perseverant exercise can even help one achieve longevity'.

此功法有歌、图二部分。歌诀是三十六句五言诗，附有小字注释。采用坐势，由叩齿、咽津、摩腰背、转肩伸脚、伸手攀足等肢体动作，结合意念活动组成。原书尚有坐位图八幅，图无名称,图下有动作说明。

Zhongli Ba Duan Jin contains verses and illustrations. As for verses, they are 36 five-word rhymes coupled with annotations. As for movements in a sitting position, these include mental focus combined with clicking the teeth, swallowing the saliva, rubbing the back and low back, rotating the shoulder, extending the leg, reaching to grasp the feet with hands, etc. Originally there are eight illustrations; however, there are no names recorded for these illustrations.

值得一提的是曾慥所撰《道枢》卷三十五《众妙篇》(见《道藏》第二十册)辑录了以文字描述的七式动作:"仰掌上举,以治三焦者也;左肝右肺如射雕焉;东西独托,所以安其脾胃矣;返复而顾,所以理其伤劳矣;大小朝天,所以通其五脏矣;咽津补气,左右挑其手,摆鳝之尾,所以祛心之疾矣;左右手以攀其足,所以治其腰矣。"

In the 35th volume (*Zhong Miao Pian,* the Chapter of Wonders) of *Dao Shu* (the Pivot of Dao) by Zeng Zao, seven movements were recorded as follows: Lift arms and turn palms to the sky to regulate Sanjiao, draw a bow to both sides to shoot a hawk, left for the liver and right for the lung, raise one hand up east and west to harmonize the spleen and stomach, look back and forward to regulate emotions, gather qi of five-zang organs to Dantian area, swallow saliva to supplement qi, flick all fingers and sweep the tail like an eel to remove heart problems and reach the feet with both hands to strengthen the low back.

南宋陈元靓所编《事林广记·修真秘旨》中载有"吕真人安乐法",所题吕真人,原指唐末著名道士吕洞宾,后人认为此系托名。其内容和《道枢·众妙篇》所辑功法基本相同，但用歌诀编成，其内容为："昂头仰托顺三焦，左肝右肺如射雕，东脾单托兼西胃，五劳回顾七伤调，脏（笔者注：脏通"鳝"）鱼摆尾通心气，两手搬脚定于腰，大小朝天安五脏，漱津咽纳指双挑。"

In the *Xiu Zhen Mi Zhi, Shi Lin Guang Ji* (the Secret of Health, the Encyclopedia) by Cheng Yuanjing in the Southern Song dynasty (1127–1279), *Lü Zhenren* (i.e., Lü Dongbin) *An Li Fa* was recorded as follows: Raise the head and lift palms to the sky to regulate Sanjiao, draw a bow to both sides to shoot a hawk, left for the liver and right for the lung, lift hand to the east to regulate the spleen and to the west to regulate the stomach, look back and forward to balance seven emotions, sweep the tail like an eel to benefit heart qi, reach the feet with both hands to strengthen the low back, gather qi of five-zang organs to Dantian area and swallow saliva and flick fingers on both hands.

此两段文字虽无"八段锦"之名，和定型的八段锦歌诀相比，二者内容较为接近，可以说是后世八段锦歌诀的原型来源之一。

Although these descriptions did not mention the name of Ba Duan Jin, they are very similar to the later verses of Ba Duan Jin and therefore considered as the prototypes of Ba Duan Jin.

早期的八段锦有站式、坐式、有单纯导引术，亦有六字气诀合导引术或吐纳兼导引等多种形式。

The early versions of Ba Duan Jin include practice in a standing/sitting position, *Dao Yin* alone, six healing sounds coupled with *Dao Yin* or *Dao Yin* coupled with *Tu Na* (inhalation and exhalation), etc.

　　明太祖朱元璋第十七子朱权（别号臞仙）撰著的《活人心法》，在《导引法》中，载录了著名的"八段锦导引法"，现存有明嘉靖二十年朝鲜刻本，尚见于《保生心鉴》（1506年）附《活人心法》、朝鲜《医方类聚·臞仙活人心》。《保生心鉴·序》谓："惟《活人心法》所刊导引八图，悉上古遗法，而为好修者宝之。"此功法是中国古导引术动静相结合的典范，在我国古代养生史与导引发展史上占有重要地位。

The well-known *Ba Duan Jin Dao Yin* method was recorded in *Huo Ren Xin Fa* (*The Method of Saving People*) by Zhu Quan (nickname: Di Xian), the 17th son of Zhu Yuanzhang (Ming Taizu, the founder and first emperor of the Ming Dynasty). Today, the Korean woodblock-printed edition completed at the 20th year (1527) of Jiajing Emperor is still available. In addition, the method was recorded in the *Bao Sheng Xin Jian* (*Personal Experience in Health Cultivation*) (1506) attached to the *Huo Ren Xin Fa* and a Korean book *Yi Fang Lei Ju · Di Xian Huo Ren Xin* (*Di Xian's Method of Saving People, Categorized Collection of Medical Formulas*). The preface of *Bao Sheng Xin Jian* states, 'the eight *Dao Yin* illustrations in the *Huo Ren Xin Fa* were passed down from remote past and cherished by those who practice'. With a perfect combination of motion (active exercises) and stillness (tranquil inner cultivation), *Ba Duan Jin Dao Yin* has played an important role in the history of Chinese Yangsheng (life-nurturing) and Dao Yin.

　　此后的明清时期多种医学和养生著作，以不同名称刊载坐式八段锦。如明代《类修要诀》"钟离祖师八段锦导引法"

（1592年）、《遵生八笺·延年却病笺》"八段锦导引法"及"八段锦坐功图"（1591年）、《夷门广牍·赤凤髓》"八段锦导引图"（1579年）、《修龄要旨》"八段锦法"（约1442年）、《摄生总要》"八段锦导引图"（1638年）、《万寿仙书》"八段锦坐功捷径"（1832年）、《三才图会》"八段锦导引图说"。

Later, the 'Zhongli (sitting) Ba Duan Jin' was referenced in many medical and health cultivation books in the Ming (1368–1644) and Qing Dynasties (1644–1912).

Books in the Ming Dynasty include *Dao Yin Fa* in the *Yi Fang Lei Ju · Di Xian Huo Ren Xin* (Di Xian's Method of Saving People, Categorized Collection of Medical Formulas), *An Mo Dao Yin* in the *Dong Yi Bao Jian · Nei Jing Pian* (Internal Medicine, Precious Mirror of Oriental Medicine) (1611), *Zhong Li Zu Shi Ba Duan Jin Dao Yin Fa* in the *Lei Xiu Yao Jue* (The Essence of Categorized Exercises) (1592), *Ba Duan Jin Dao Yin F*a and *Ba Duan Jin Zuo Gong Tu* in the *Zun Sheng Ba Jian · Yan Nian Que Bing Jian* (Achieving Longevity and Removing Diseases, Health Cultivation in Eight Ways) (1591), *Ba Duan Jin Dao Yin Tu* in the *Yi Men Guang Du · Chi Feng Sui* (Marrow of Red Phoenix, Archives By a Hermit) (1579), *Ba Duan Jin Fa* in the *Xiu Ling Yao Zhi* (The Essence of Health Cultivation Exercise) (approximately 1642) and *Ba Duan Jin Dao Yin Tu* in the *She Sheng Zong Yao* (General Principle for Health Cultivation) (1638), *Ba Duan Jin Zuo Gong Jie Jing* in the *Wan Shou Xian Shu* (Treatises on Longevity and Immortality) (1632) and *Ba Duan Jin Dao Yin Tu Shuo* in the *San Cai Tu Hui* (Assembled Illustrations of Heaven, Earth and Man).

清代《心医集》"八段锦"和"八段锦诗"（1656年）、《颐养诠要》"钟离公八段锦"（1705年）、《养生秘旨》"八段导引法"（1891年）、《内外功图说辑要》下集"八段锦内功"（1918年）

和"八段锦口诀解要"(1920年);朝鲜《医方类聚·駒仙活人心》"导引法"(1445年)、《东医宝鉴·内景篇》"按摩导引"(1611年),都引用八段锦歌诀或坐功图,掀起了明清导引大发展的热潮。

Books in the Qing Dynasty include *Ba Duan Jin* and *Ba Duan Jin Poem* in the *Xin Yi Ji* (Zhu Dengyuan's Experience in Health Cultivation Exercise) (1656), *Zhongli Gong Ba Duan Jin* in the *Yi Yang Quan Yao* (Elaboration Summary of Health Conservation) (1705), *Da Duan Dao Yin Fa* in the *Yang Sheng Mi Zhi* (Secret Tips on Health Cultivation) (1891), *Ba Duan Jin Nei Gong* in the second part of *Nei Wei Gong Tu Shuo Ji Yao* (Summary of Illustrated Internal and External Exercises) (1918), and *Ba Duan Jin Kou Jue Jie Yao* (Elaborations on Verses of Ba Duan Jin) (1920).

除了上述坐式八段锦歌诀外,尚有不同的八段锦歌诀流传,明代胡文焕《类修要诀》引用《灵剑子引导子午记·引导诀》,并将其改名为"许真君引导诀";朝鲜金礼蒙等编集的《医方类聚》辑录了南宋的"吕真人安乐法";清代冯曦(字晴川,号汉炜、守和道人)所撰《颐养诠要》收载了"吕祖安乐歌",与南宋的"吕真人安乐法"较为接近。清代娄杰(字受之)尝从山左徐君学八段锦立功,数年后又得坐功,经数十年研习,颇有心得,于清光绪二年(1876年)编撰《八段锦坐立功法图诀》,书中图文兼备,现有清光绪二年芳草轩刻本。清末青莱真人撰《八段锦图说》,清广州守经堂刻本。近代流传最广的动功八段锦套路,定型的八段锦歌诀,据唐豪考证,均发生在清光绪年间。清光绪十六年(1890年)上海同文书局出版的托名梁世昌《幼学操身》,清光绪二十四年(1898年)刊行的《新出保身图说·八段锦图》,两书所载的八句七言歌诀为早期版本。其七言歌诀为:"两手托天理三焦,左右开弓似射雕。调理脾胃须单举,五劳七伤往后瞧。摇头摆尾去心火,背后七颠百病消。攒拳怒目增气力，两手攀足固肾腰。"

Historically, there are other recordings of Ba Duan Jin verses. The *Lei Xiu Yao Jue* (The Essence of Categorized Exercises) in the Ming Dynasty cited *Ling Jian Zi Yin Dao Zi Wu Ji · Yin Dao Jue* and renamed it '*Xu Zhen Jun Yin Dao Jue*'. The *Yi Fang Lei Ju* (Categorized Collection of Medical Formulas) by Jin Li-meng from Korea recorded '*Lü Zhen Ren (i.e. Lü Dong-bin) An Le Fa*'. The *Yi Yang Quan Yao* (Elaboration Summary of Health Conservation) by Feng Xi (courtesy name Qing Chuan, pseudonym Han Wei or Shou He Dao Ren) in the Qing Dynasty recorded similar '*Lü Zu (i.e. Lü Dong-bin) An Le Ge*'. After studying Ba Duan Jin in both standing and sitting positions, Lou Jie (courtesy name Shou Zhi) in the Qing Dynasty compiled the *Ba Duan Jin Zuo Li Gong Fa Tu Jue* (Illustrated Ba Duan Jin Verses in Standing and Sitting Positions) in 1876 (the 2nd year of Guangxu era). Today, *Fang Cao Xuan* woodblock-printed edition (1876) of this book is still available, coupled with the Guangzhou Shou Jing Tang woodblock-printed edition of *Ba Duan Jin Tu Shuo* (Illustrated Ba Duan Jin) by Qing Lai Zhen Ren in the Qing Dynasty. According to the textual research by Tang Hao[1], most popular dynamic Ba Duan Jin movements and verses were formed in the Guangxu period. The *You Xue Cao Shen* (Physical Exercises for Children) published by Shanghai Tongwen Shuju[2] in 1890 and the *Xin Chu Bao Shen Tu · Ba Duan Jin Tu* (Ba Duan Jin movements in Illustrated New Methods for Health Preservation) published in 1898 recorded the following 7-character verse:

Lifting the Heavens with Two Hands to Regulate *Sanjiao*

1. Tang Hao (1887–1959): a Chinese lawyer and expert on Chinese martial arts. He published a dozen books on the history of Chinese martial arts.
2. Tongwen Shuju: the first lithographic printing house in the history of China, founded by Xu Xun and Xu Hong-fu in 1882. Unfortunately, it was closed in 1898.

Drawing the Bow Both Left and Right-Handed to Shoot the Hawk

Holding One Arm Aloft to Regulate the Spleen and Stomach

Looking from Side to Side to Prevent Five Overstrains and Seven Injuries[1]

Swaying the Head and Shaking to Clear Heart-Fire

7 Times of Bouncing to Relieve All Diseases

Clenching the Fists and Glaring Angrily to Increase Strength

Holding the Feet with Both Hands to Consolidate the Kidney and Low Back

此歌诀与明清流行的八段锦歌诀相比，去掉了呼吸吐纳、意守丹田等意念内容，在继承《灵剑子引导子午记·引导诀》的基础上，强化了肢体导引部分，面向大众，使初学者易于学习。歌诀问世后，成为近现代最有影响的一种歌诀。后世把坐式、立式，分别称为坐八段、立八段。立八段又有文武、南北之分。锻炼时多采用马步，动作刚劲，称为武八段或北派；锻炼时多采用站式，动作柔和，称为文八段或南派。

Compared with the verses in the Ming and Qing dynasties, this verse is easier to learn and has become the most influential one, since it removed breathing in, breathing out and mental focus on Dantian and highlighted physical movements on the basis of *Ling Jian Zi Yin Dao Zi Wu Ji · Yin Dao Jue*. Later, Ba Duan Jin in sitting and standing positions are named Sitting Ba Duan Jin and Standing Ba Duan Jin. Further to this classification,

---

1. Five overstrains refer to damages to the liver, heart, spleen, lung and kidney; they may also refer to five causes of overstrains: long-time use of your eyes damages your blood, long-time sitting damages your muscles, long-term standing damages your bones, long-time walking damages your tendons and long-time bed rest damages your qi. Seven injuries refer to negative effects caused by extreme emotions such as joy, anger, worry, grief, sadness, fear and fright.

standing Ba Duan Jin is subdivided into the Northern school and Southern School. The northern school, also known as the hard style, involves horse riding stance and tough movements; while the southern school, also known as the soft style, involves standing posture and gentle movements.

1957年人民体育出版社出版了《八段锦》一书，书中简要叙述了八段锦对人体的作用、锻炼要领，并根据定型的八段锦歌诀，图文并茂地详述由卓大宏、马凤阁、唐豪所编的三套立式和马凤阁所编的一套坐式的八段锦功法。内容通俗易懂，发行量极大，为八段锦的普及推广作出了贡献。

The *Ba Duan Jin* published by the People's Sports Publishing House of China in 1957 described the functions and practice tips of Ba Duan Jin and illustrated three sets of standing Ba Duan Jin by Zhuo Da-hong, Ma Feng-ge and Tang Hao and one set of sitting Ba Duan Jin by Ma Feng-ge. With a huge number of printed copies, this easy-to-understand book has greatly contributed to the popularization and promotion of Ban Duan Jin.

又有少林寺八段锦，关于八段锦的起源，认为是由《易筋经》演化而来，相传达摩祖师于中国南朝梁武帝时期从印度航海到广州，至南朝都城建业会梁武帝，面谈不契，遂一苇渡江，北上北魏都城洛阳，后卓锡嵩山少林寺，面壁九年，《易筋经》就是当年所留。由于《易筋经》过于专业，动作难度大，修炼时间太长，少林高僧就从其中抽出八个动作，集锦而成，故名八段锦。

Some scholars believe Ba Duan Jin originated from Shaolin[1]

1. Shaolin often refers to the *Shaolin* Monastery, or Shaolin Temple, a Buddhist monastery in Henan province, China. Specifically, it refers to *Shaolin* Kung Fu, the school of martial arts associated with the monastery.

*Yi Jin Jing* (Sinew Transforming Classic). As the old legend goes, Bodhidharma (from India) arrived in Guangzhou by sea in the era of Emperor Wu of the Southern Liang Dynasty (502–557). After a brief and unsuccessful meeting with the emperor in Jianye (today's Nanjing in Jiangsu Province), Bodhidharma was said to have crossed the river on a single stem of reed, travelled north to Luoyang, the capital of the Northern Wei Dynasty (386–534) and settled at the Shaolin Temple on Mount Song, where he sat facing a wall without a word for nine years and finally created the *Yi Jin Jing*. Since *Yi Jin Jing* is difficult to learn, the Shaolin monks selected eight movements and named these movements Ba Duan Jin.

在少林寺《易筋经外经图说·外壮练力奇验图》(清代，佚名)、《八段锦体操图 (12式)》当中都比较详细地讲解了八段锦。在少林功法发展的过程中，少林高僧经过自己的刻苦修习，逐渐将历史上流传的八段锦和少林寺禅修，少林特有功法以及中医阴阳五行藏象、经络腧穴学说相结合，形成了别有特色的少林八段锦，僧人将其作为健身养生的方法和武术基本功来练习，强身健体、疗疾康复的效果更加明显。

*Ba Duan Jin* was clearly explained in detail in the *Yi Jin Jing Wai Jing Tu Shuo · Wai Zhuang Lian Li Qi Yan Tu* (Amazing Experience in Building Physical Strength, Illustrations of Yi Jin Jing Branches) (unknown author in Qing Dynasty) and *Ba Duan Jin Ti Cao Tu* (Gymnastic Illustrations of 12 Ba Duan Jin Movements). Along with the evolution of Shaolin Kung Fu (martial arts), Shaolin monks created their special Shaolin Ba Duan Jin by integrating Ba Duan Jin, Shaolin meditation and Shaolin martial arts with Chinese medical theories on yin, yang, five elements, internal organs and meridians & points. Buddhist monks practice Shaolin Ba Duan Jin as part of their daily training to preserve health, improve their martial arts skills and recover from injuries.

---

又道家秘传八段锦者，乃"拔断筋"之别名，是道家配合静功修炼的动功，又名"千八攒除疾道功"。因道家前辈先贤练此功是想拔断俗筋（变化气质，脱胎换骨之谓），以救静坐气滞血枯之弊。而千八攒之名是说需习练一千八百把才有显著效验。此功法见录于《武术汇宗》，作者是近代武学大师万籁声。万籁声先生于20世纪20年代得自于北京白云观隐士王显斋。该功法以"天人合一"的道家理论为依据，以人体为一小周天，暗合天地、宇宙之星相，以日月、青龙、白虎、朱雀、玄武对应动作。其动作简单，但蕴涵至深，运动柔和，流畅，连续不断。该功法为手臂绕身体前、后、左、右、上、下运动，配合头部转动以及每一动作均配合腿部有节奏的轻微屈伸，故对于中老年肩周炎，颈椎病、腰腿病能起到很好的改善功效；另外千八攒的"攒"为握拳，故每个动作中均有握拳，手部常握拳，可对应增强心、肺等内脏器官的功能，对于延缓内脏功能衰退有很好的效果；动作柔和，连续不断，使气血运行流畅，疏通经脉。故长期坚持练习该功法，必会通过简单的动作，达到健身的效果。

Some scholars believe *Ba Duan Jin* is another name of *Ba Duan Jin* (literally means Extreme Stretching of the Sinew) or *Qian Ba Zan Chu Ji Dao Gong* (Disease-Removing Daoist Exercise by Repeating 1,800 Times, indicating that it takes lots of practice to obtain remarkable effects), an active physical exercise in combination with tranquil inner cultivation. Daoist sages practiced this to stretch and transform sinew to compensate for the qi stagnation and blood exhaustion due to long-term sitting meditation. This exercise method was quoted in the *Wu Shu Hui Zong* (Collections of Martial Arts) by Wan Lai-sheng, a prominent 20th- century martial artist who learned from Wang Xian-zhai, a hermit at the Baiyun (White Cloud) Daoist Temple in Beijing.

Based on the Daoist theory of 'harmony between man and nature', this exercise uses the body as a smaller heavenly cycle (microcosmic orbit), coincides with astrology of the world and universe and adopts movements corresponding to sun, moon, green dragon, white tiger, vermillion bird and black tortoise. These profound movements are simple, gentle, smooth and continuous. Characterized by arm circling the front, back, left, right, upper part and lower part of the body, coupled with head rotation and rhythmic mild flexion and extension of the leg, this exercise can alleviate frozen shoulder and pain in the neck, low back and leg in middle-aged and elderly people. In addition, the word 'Zan' (*Qian Ba Zan Chu Ji Dao Gong*) means clenching a fist in each movement, which can benefit the heart and lung. Gentle smooth and continuous movements allow free flow of qi and blood in meridians. As a result, regular practice of these simple movements can promote health.

上海市气功研究所在以"精气神"为基础，以《黄帝内经》之"正气存内，邪不可干""恬淡虚无，真气从之"为宗旨，糅合各家八段锦，经过十数年研习、临床研究，尤其注重心性变化，气质改变；具体动作以神意为先，骨肉为辅。适用于修身养性，延年祛病。

Based on essence (*Jing*), qi and spirit (*Shen*) as well as the theory 'when there is sufficient healthy qi inside, the pathogenic qi have no way to invade the body' and 'genuine qi will be with you when you achieve *Tian* (peaceful joy), *Dan* (no greed for fame and wealth), *Xu* (void) and *Wu* (nothingness)' in the *Huang Di Nei Jing* (Yellow Emperor's Inner Classic)[1],

---

1. An ancient Chinese medical text that has been treated as the fundamental doctrinal source for Chinese medicine for more than two millennia, the work is composed of two texts — *Su Wen* (Basic Questions) and *Ling Shu* (Spiritual Pivot).

staff at the Shanghai Qigong Research Institute revised Ba Duan Jin through decades of practice and clinical studies. They especially attached much importance to one's character, quality and temperament. As for specific body movements, mental intention comes first. Consequently the revised Ba Duan Jin can help to nurture one's character, remove diseases and achieve health and longevity.

八　段　锦　·　*Ba Duan Jin*

## Theoretical Foundation

理论基础

以单纯形体动作而言，八段锦的效果和广播操、自我保健按摩作用类似。其所能产生修身养性、祛病延年的作用完全在于神意、精气的参与、净化、升华。而要理解神与精、心性与气，一定离不开经典传统文化的基本理论概念，练功需明理，最忌盲修瞎练如盲人骑瞎马，夜半临深渊。

In terms of functions of body movements alone, *Ba Duan Jin* is similar to broadcast gymnastics and self-care massage. However, mental intention and essential qi are crucial to its function in nurturing one's character and promoting health. To fully understand spirit, essence, character and qi, one needs first to be familiar with basic concepts in traditional culture. In other words, one needs to understand the underlying truth before practice Ba Duan Jin. Otherwise, it's like 'a blind man riding a blind horse approaches the brink of an unfathomable pool at midnight'.

# 明 理 之 路

## The Way to Pursue Underlying Truth

传统文化理论体系与现代科学完全不同。现代科学是以"物"为研究对象来寻求科学至理，故极重"物证"。而传统文化的底蕴是"道"——宇宙，生命，一切之根本。"物"是"道"的显现——"相"，无时无刻地在迁延变化。

The theoretical system of traditional culture is totally different from that of modern science. Modern science aims to pursue truth or knowledge of phenomena of the 'physical world' and therefore highlights 'physical evidence'; whereas traditional culture focuses on 'Dao'— the underlying natural order of the universe. The phenomena of the 'physical world' are just the manifestation of 'Dao'— a 'phase' that changes all the time.

道（无）→太极（有），道——宇宙的本体，最基本的规律，《道德经》上说，有物混然而成，在天地形成以前就已经存在。听不到它的声音也看不见它的形体，寂静而空灵，不依靠任何外力而独立存在，循环运行而永不衰竭，可以作为万物的根本，我不知道它的名字，所以勉强把它叫做道。《老子》云：无名天地之始；有名万物之母。《老子》亦云：道生一，一生二，二生三，三生万物矣。道（无极）之中自然而然，法尔如是地蕴育，转化，产生太极——真灵一气；太极一气自然含有阴阳二气，阴阳和合变化则万物生长老死。

Dao can be thought of as the flow of the universe. The basic law of Dao is to transform from nothingness to existence. The *Dao De Jing*[1] states, 'There was something undefined and complete, coming into existence before Heaven and Earth. We look at it, and we do not see it. We listen to it, and we do not hear it. How still it was and formless, standing alone, and undergoing no change, reaching everywhere and in no danger of being exhausted! It may be regarded as the Mother of all things. I do not know its name, and I give it the designation of the Dao'. This text says, 'Conceived of as having no name, it is the Originator of heaven and earth; conceived of as having a name, it is the Mother of all things', and 'the Dao produced One; One produced Two; Two produced Three; Three produced All things'. The law of the Dao is its being what it is.

1. Also simply referred to as the Laozi, is a Chinese classic text. According to tradition, it was written around 6th century BC by the sage Laozi.

《黄帝内经素问·天元纪大论》曰："太虚寥廓,肇基化元,万物资始。五运终天,布气真灵,揔统坤元。九星悬朗,七曜周旋,曰阴曰阳,曰柔曰刚,幽显既位,寒暑弛张,生生化化,品物咸章。"

无边无际的太虚(道),是宇宙造化的原始基础,是万物化生的根本。其间五运往复循行,真灵之气遍布,主宰着一切生命生长的根源。由此九星明朗地悬耀于虚空,七曜循着天道有规律地运行,于是天运有了阴阳的迁移变化,大地有了刚柔的生杀现象,昼夜有了幽暗和明亮的变化,四时有了寒暑的更迭,如此不断生长变化,才有了丰富多样的万物生长。

Chapter 66 of the *Huang Di Nei Jing Su Wen* states, 'the extension of the Great Void is boundless; it is the basis of all founding and it is the principal source of all transformation. The myriad beings depend on the Great Void to come into existence, and it is because of the Great Void that the five movements (*Wu Yun*) complete their course in heaven. The Great Void spreads the true magic power of qi, and it exerts control over the principal qi of the earth. Hence the nine stars are suspended in heaven and shine and the seven luminaries revolve in a cycle. This is called yin; this is called yang. This is called soft; this is called hard. Hence when that which is in the dark and that which is obvious have assumed their positions, there is cold and summer-heat, tension and relaxation. Generation follows upon generation, transformation follows upon transformation, with the result that all the things come into open existence.'

在传统道家文化思想中可以把此理论体系概括为:道(体)→气(化)→物(变);与现代科学观点不同,认为在物质之前还有气与道的变化。《医门法律》"气聚则形成,气散则形亡"。最有意思的典故当属"庄子丧妻",庄子妻子死了,惠子来吊丧,庄子正盘膝而坐敲击瓦盆唱歌。惠子说:与妻子共居,孩子大了,她也老迈了,现在死了不哭也已足够,又敲击瓦盆唱歌,不是太过分了吗!庄子说:不是这样。在她刚死的时候,我难道能不悲痛么!然而推究其最初本来是未曾有生命,不但未曾有生命,而且本来没有形体;不但没有形体,而且本来无气。在恍惚迷离状态中,变化而有了气,气化而有形体,形体变而有生命。现在又由生而变成死,这就像那春秋冬夏四季交替运行一样。假如有人安稳地睡在大房子里,而我在旁边哭泣不止,自以为这样做是不通达天命的,所以停止哭祭。

From the perspective of traditional Daoist culture, the above theoretical system can be summarized into Dao (natural order) →qi (transformation) →physical world (changes). Unlike modern scientific view, Daoism believes there are changes of qi and Dao before the material world. The *Yi Men Fa Lù* (Precepts for Medical Practice) (1658) says, 'When qi gathers, the physical body is formed; when qi disperses, the body dies'. This can be best explained from the following story *Zhuang Zi's wife died.*

When Zhuangzi's wife died, Hui Shi came to condole. As for Zhuangzi, he was squatting with his knees out, drumming on a pot and singing. "When you have lived with someone," said Hui Shi, "and brought up children, and grown old together, to refuse to bewail her death would be bad enough, but to drum on a pot and sing — could there be anything more shameful?" "Not so. When she first died, do you suppose that I was able not to feel the loss? I peered back into her beginnings; there was a time before there was a life. Not only was there no life, there was at time before there was a shape. Not only was there no shape, there was a time before there was energy. Mingled together in the amorphous, something altered, and there was the energy; by the alteration in the energy there was the shape, by alteration of the shape there was the life. Now once more altered, she has gone over to death. This is to be companion with spring and autumn, summer and winter, in the procession of the four seasons. When someone was about to lie down and sleep in the greatest of mansions, I with my sobbing knew no better than to bewail her. The thought came to me that I was being uncomprehending towards destiny, so I stopped weeping."

此道（体）→气（化）→物（变）理论体系与现代科学完全不同，此理论之最基本元素、最重要元素是道。气（化）、物（变）无非是道的变数而已。故而首先重悟道、合乎道，其次明了变化的规律，而否定一切片面孤立、固定不变的"物的存在"。若以重"物证"之思维模式去研究传统文化中之"道""理"，无异于南辕北辙。

Apparently, Dao is the most fundamental element in the above theoretical system; and qi (transformation) and physical world (changes) are different forms of Dao. Therefore, it is important to comprehend and follow the Dao. Otherwise, it's like 'going south by driving the chariot north (doing something counterproductive to one's goal)' to study 'Dao' and 'Logic' in traditional culture from the mindset of 'physical evidence'.

习练八段锦等传统养生术，本质上是返本还源：物（变）→气（化）→道（体），其注重的是"净化，升华"，在这一过程中才有可能讨论"精、气、神"，"心性←→气"。

In essence, traditional health cultivation practice including Ba Duan Jin tends to return to the origin: physical world (changes) →qi (transformation) →Dao (natural order). They stress more on 'cleansing and uplifting' process, in which the essence, qi and spirit or temperament⟷qi are discussed.

# 真 气 的 由 来
## The Origin of Zhen (Genuine) Qi

气功追求的是"真气、正气","真气、正气"与"道"、"德"戚戚相关。

Qigong practice pursues Zhen (genuine) qi and Zheng (healthy/positive) qi, which are closely associated with 'Dao' and 'De' (virtue).

道：宇宙的本体，最基本的规律。《系辞传》："一阴一阳之谓道"、"天之道，曰阴与阳"；孔子："形而上者谓之道，形而下者谓之器"，所以说"道者，阴阳变化之理也"。

Dao is the underlying natural order of the universe. The *Zhou Yi*[1] *Xi Ci* (Philosophical interpretation on the Book of Changes) states, 'One Yin and One Yang are called Dao' and 'the Dao of heaven is known as yin and yang'. Confucius believed 'what is above the form (metaphysical) is called Dao; what is under the form (physical) is called a tool'. As a result, 'Dao is the interaction between yin and yang'.

德：心性中内在的本质。《孟子》："恻隐之心，人皆有之；羞恶之心，人皆有之；恭敬之心，人皆有之；是非之心，人皆有之。恻隐之心，仁也；羞恶之心，义也；恭敬之心，礼也；是非之

---

1. An ancient divination text and the oldest of the Chinese classics.

心，智也。仁义礼智，非由外铄我固有之也，弗思耳矣。"同情心属于仁；羞耻心属于义；恭敬心属于礼；是非心属于智。这仁、义、礼、智都不是由外在的因素加给我的，而是我本身固有的，只不过平时没有去想它因而不觉得罢了。

De (virtue) is the inherent nature or character. The *Mengzi* (Mencius) states, 'the feeling of commiseration is essential to man, that the feeling of shame and dislike is essential to man, that the feeling of modesty and complaisance is essential to man, and that the feeling of approving and disapproving is essential to man.' The feeling of commiseration is the principle of benevolence. The feeling of shame and dislike is the principle of righteousness. The feeling of modesty and complaisance is the principle of propriety. The feeling of approving and disapproving is the principle of knowledge. Men have these four principles just as they have their four limbs. Yet, they just do not realize they have them'.

"道德"二字连用始于荀子《劝学》篇："故学至乎礼而止矣，夫是之谓道德之极。"现代文中"道德"一般指一种社会意识形态，它是人们共同生活及其行为的准则和规范。所以传统文化中"道德"的语义远比此更深刻、更丰富。

Dao and De were first used in combination in the *Quan Xue* (the chapter of 'Persuading/Encouraging Learning') by Xun Zi[1] as '... therefore learning reaches its completion with the rituals, for they may be said to represent the highest point of *Dao De* (inner strength/personal character)'. Today, 'Dao De' is a social ideology, referring to a body of standards or principles derived from a code of conduct. It can be seen that the word 'Dao De' in traditional culture is far more profound than in modern text.

---

1. Along with Confucius and Mencius, Xun Zi was one of the three great early architects of Confucian philosophy.

# 气的基本概念
## Basic Concept of Qi

气是构成宇宙、人体、维持人体生命活动的最基本元素。气还可以从能量，功能性来理解。

Qi is the most essential substance that constitutes the universe and human body and acts to maintain vital activities. It can be understood from energy and functions.

### 1. 能量
### 1. Energy

能量指清气、水谷精微之气、元气等。清气，比如城市中久住，忽然换到一个空气特别清新的地方，人就会精神振奋，这是因为人通过肺获得天地之间气的能量。水谷精微之气，人可以通过肠胃从食物中分清泌浊获得必需能量。元气，先天禀赋，比如有的小孩生来多病，有的强健有力，有的聪慧敏捷，有的稍稍迟钝，皆因禀赋所致。

Energy here includes clean qi, nutrients qi from water and grains and yuan-primordial qi. An example can help us understand clean qi. After living in a city for a long period of time, we feel refreshed when we travel to a place with fresh air, because we breathed in fresh air from the nature through our lung. As for nutrients qi, we need energy from water and food through our stomach and intestines. Yuan-primordial qi is inherited from one's parents, just like some kids are born weak, some strong, some smart and some relatively dull.

## 2. 功能性
## 2. Functions

功能性指气机、神机、神意,具有调节功能。比如怒则气上,人发怒生气脸红脖子粗,血压上升,气之所致。

Functions of qi include qi activity, vital activity, mental intention and regulation. For example, anger causes qi to ascend, leading to a red face and elevated blood pressure.

以上所述之气,皆局部、有限之气,并非养生气功所求,气功追求的是"真气、正气","真气、正气"与"道"、"德"戚戚相关。所谓"正气存内,邪不可干","恬淡虚无,真气从之"。"真气、正气"的获得离不开道德的修养。《道德经》:"道生之,德畜之,物形之,势成之。是以万物莫不尊道而贵德。道之尊,德之贵,夫莫之命而常自然。""道"和"德"为"生长万物"和"畜养万物"。《庄子》的《天地篇》就说:"通于天地者,德也;行于万物者,道也。"并称:"形非道不生,生非德不明。存形穷生,立德明道,非至德者邪?"《孟子》则说,我善于培养自己的浩然正气……这种气,极其浩大,极其有力量,用正直去培养它而不加以伤害,就会充满天地之间。不过,这种气必须与仁义道德相配,否则就会缺乏力量。而且,必须要有经常性的仁义道德蓄养才能生成,而不是靠偶尔的正义行为就能获取的。一旦你的行为问心有愧,这种气就会缺乏力量了。

However, the aforementioned qi is not the 'qi' we pursued in qigong practice. As we mentioned before, qigong practice pursues Zhen (genuine) qi and Zheng (healthy/positive) qi that are closely associated with 'Dao' and 'De (virtue)'. This is what we say 'when there is sufficient healthy qi inside, the pathogenic qi have no way to invade the body' and 'genuine qi will be with you when you achieve (peaceful joy), Dan (no greed for fame and wealth), Xu (void) and Wu (nothingness)'. To acquire Zhen qi and Zheng qi, we need to follow Dao and cultivate our virtue. The *Dao De Jing* states, 'All things are produced by the Dao, and nourished by the De (virtue). They receive their forms according to the nature of each, and are completed according to the circumstances of their condition. Therefore all things without exception honor the Dao, and exalt the virtue. This honoring of the Dao and exalting of its operation is not the result of any ordination, but always a spontaneous tribute'. In summary, 'Dao' produces all things and 'De' nourishes all things. The outer chapter *Heaven and Earth* in *Zhuangzi* states, 'pervading heaven and earth, that is the Dao; moving among the ten thousand things, that is the De'. This chapter also states, 'Without Dao, the body can have no life. Without De, life can have no clarity. To preserve the body and live out life, to establish De and clarify Dao—is this not kingly (De) virtue'? Mencius says, 'I'm good at nourishing my flood-like righteous qi ...' He goes on to describe what means by 'flood-like righteous qi': It is the sort of qi utmost in vastness and power. If, by uprightness, you nourish it and do not interfere with it, it fills the space between Heaven and Earth. It is the sort of qi that matches virtue and morality; without these, it starves. It is generated by the accumulation of virtue and morality — one cannot attain it by sporadic righteousness. If anything one does fails to meet the standards of one's heart-mind, it starves.

　　我们现在所习练的八段锦以"恬淡虚无，真气从之"为宗旨。恬、淡、虚、无，由浅入深，是与道相合的四种境界。恬：宁静安详快乐（舒坦松快自在）。这种快乐与外物的得失无关，由内在自然地升起。淡：淡泊。淡泊以明志，宁静以致远。虚：无两种境界就更难解释，姑且作个比喻，人处房中，掩门关窗，拉上厚绒窗帘，此时伸手不见五指，比喻普通人之常态。拉开窗帘，此时阳光照进屋子，透过玻璃，外面的景色清晰可见，象征第一层境界"恬"；打开门窗，内外相通，象征第二层境界"淡"；人在屋中，把房拆尽，内外一体，象征第三层境界"虚"；人亦不存，象征第四层"无"。

The principle of our revised Ba Duan Jin lies in the 'genuine qi will be with you when you achieve Tian (peaceful joy), Dan (no greed for fame and wealth), Xu (void) and Wu (nothingness)'. *Tian*, *Dan*, *Xu* and *Wu* are four levels of following the Dao. *Tian* means tranquil, serene and joyful. This peaceful joy arises from the inner heart and has nothing to do with gain and loss in real life. *Dan* means not to seek fame and wealth. One can only determine his/her aspiration by not seeking secular fame and wealth; one can only achieve his/her ambition by having a tranquil peaceful mind. *Xu and Wu* are more difficult to explain. These four levels can be explained from the following example (metaphor). Imagine you are in a room with a closed door, windows and thick wool curtain. You cannot see your own fingers in this dark room. This is a normal state of ordinary people. When the curtain is pulled aside, the sunlight enters the room, allowing you to see the scene outside through the window. This is the first level '*Tian*'. When the door and windows are open, you feel the room is connected with the outside world. This is the second level of '*Dan*'. When you are still in the room but feel like the house is absent, this is the third level of 'Xu (void)'. When you forget yourself, this is the fourth level of 'Wu (nothingness)'.

练功只有入境（静），寂然不动，感而遂通，打破小我，方能与天地大道之真气融会贯通。借用朱熹的小诗：半亩方塘一鉴开，天光云影共徘徊。问渠哪得清如许？为有源头活水来。

During qigong practice, to connect with the Zhen (genuine)

qi between the heaven and earth, you need to forget yourself in tranquil stillness. This can be vividly reflected in a poem by Zhu Xi[1]:

A small square pond an uncovered mirror

Where sunlight and clouds linger and leave

I asked how it stays so clear

It said spring water keeps flowing in

练习气功就是不断地追求生命宇宙真谛,犹如天之精神,《易经》云: 天行健,君子自强不息。练习气功就是要勇于承担起生命的大任,亦如大地般的德行,《易》云: 地道坤厚,德以载物。

Through qigong practice, we can seek the truth about our life and universe. Through qigong practice, we are willing to assume responsibility of our life. The *Yi Jing* (*Zhou Yin*, Book of Changes) states, 'As Heaven keeps vigor through movement, a gentleman should unremittingly practice self-improvement. As the earth bears everything on it, a gentleman should generously cultivate to become tolerant'.

# 与现代体育锻炼差异

## Differences between Ba Duan Jin Practice and Modern Physical Exercise

### 1. 教授方式不同

### 1. Difference in Teaching Method

传统功法教授注重因材施教,因机施教。每一个人的体质

---

1. A Song Dynasty Confucian scholar who became the leading figure of the School of Principle and the most influential rationalist Neo-Confucian in China.

秉性，生活习惯等不同，就算是同一套功法，有的人可以从静入手，有的人可以从动入手，有从"精"入手，有从"气"入手，有从"神"入手；又有对传统思想体悟的深浅不同，天赋差异，可以直接从整体（道）入手，可以从局部入手，可以从无为入手，可以从有为入手，可以以神意为先，也可以从肢体开始。

Student tailored teaching methods are often adopted in traditional qigong learning. Considering from individualized constitution and lifestyles, even for same exercise, some can begin with static meditation, some with active body movements, some with 'essence', some with 'qi' and some with 'spirit'. Due to differences in gift and knowledge in traditional culture, some can begin with the whole (Dao), some with a part, some with inaction, some with action, some with mental intention and some with body movements.

所有一切又以师为最重。老师以体悟之道，身体力行之经验，根据学生禀赋、心性，从最初的接引，路途中的引导与磨砺，最后的印证，都是老师的心血汇聚。在传统文化中老师的重要性是第一位的。

Above all, teachers play the most important role in learning traditional qigong exercise. Experience, guidance and instruction of teachers are extremely significant.

### 2. 动作要领、要求不同
### 2. Difference in Key Principles and Movement Requirements

现代体育锻炼等在科学理论的框架下，一般对动作要求标准化、统一化。

传统养生术中往往一套功法，由于流派的不同，具体动作差异很大，即使同一个老师，不同的学生间动作都有差异。这是因为传统功法讲究动作，但更注重心法传承——每一个传统流派都有理论体系、气血运行等练功的窍要所在。由于每个人对传统思想的理解与体悟不同，男女差别，年龄身体变化，故而没有一个"绝对到位，固定不变"的动作，只有符合心法的合适的动作。

However, traditional health cultivation practice varies greatly between different schools. Movements may also vary among students even though they learn from the same teacher, since traditional qigong practice focuses more on mental intention than specific movements. Due to differences in understanding the underlying idea, gender and age, there are appropriate movements instead of fixed, standardized ones.

### 3. 理论体系不同
### 3. Difference in Theoretical System

现代体育锻炼、健身操、康复操依据人体解剖、生理、生化指标等科学理论。

Modern physical exercise, body building exercise and recuperative gymnastics are based on human anatomy, physiology and biochemical indices.

传统养生术以道（生）→气（化）→物（变）为理论核心，以阴阳变化为纲领,以五脏经络气血运行为指导,配合天时、地利,以中和平衡为目的。

Based on Dao (natural order) →qi (transformation) →physical world (changes), yin-yang changes, five-zang organs, circulation of qi and blood along meridians, traditional health cultivation practice aims to achieve moderation and balance through exercise in the right place at the right time.

Characteristics and Essential Principles

特色与要领

# 灵动生命活力

## Living a Vigorous Life

一般认为"养生"就是"健身"，身体健康就对了。中医注重身心的平衡，不仅仅只关心肉体的"身"。传统养生术养的是"生"，何谓"生"？即生命中最原始，灵动生命活力——"生气"，而此肉体之"身"只不过是"生气"的具象表现形式而已。那么"生气"又源于哪里呢？《黄帝内经素问·至真要大论》"天地之纪，人神之通应"；《黄帝内经素问·天元纪大论》"在天为气，在地成形，形气相感而化生万物"，指出人与天道相应。"生气"源于道。道与人本质为一，如果孤立、片面、执着看待事物，那么人与道现象上为二，就好比一杯水与大海，本质是水，一杯水离开大海迟早会蒸发，而杯水溶入海，杯水即是海，海亦如杯水。人之"生气"与"天道"，犹如"杯水"与"海"。人若悟道，便晓"杯水即是海"；人若了道，即晓"海亦如杯水"。所以在传统文化思想中那些先贤与大德们才会有"生者寄也，死者归矣""生死一如"之说。

It's generally believed that *Yang Sheng* (Nurturing Life) means physical fitness. However, in addition to physical body, Chinese medicine highlights body-mind balance. When we say nurturing life, we mean the most original vigor of life—vital qi. Physical body is just a concrete manifestation of vital qi. What is the origin of 'vital qi'? Chapter 74 of the *Huang Di Nei Jing* states, 'seasonal changes of the nature correspond with changes inside the human body'. Chapter 66 of the *Huang Di Nei Jing* states, 'In heaven it is qi; on the earth it turns into physical appearance. Physical appearance and qi affect each other and thereby they generate, through transformation, the myriad beings'. As a result, the vital qi originates from Dao. In nature, Dao and man are one. If things are looked at in an isolated, partial and obsessive way, man and Dao will be separated into two. This can be explained from a glass of water and the ocean. In nature, a glass of water and the ocean are water. The glass of water will evaporate if it's separated from the ocean. When the glass of water is poured into the sea, they become one. Dao of the heaven is to vital qi what the ocean is to the glass of water. If we understand Dao, we know 'the glass of water is the ocean'; if we are with the Dao, we know 'the ocean is the glass of water'. In traditional culture, sages and men with great virtue believed 'Life is a dream walking; death is a going home' and 'Death is just a part of the life circulation, so the death is the birth'.

"养生"绝不是贪生恶死，传统养生思想注重"生"，诚如夫子言"未知生焉知死"。活着才能彻悟此天地之道，才能与道相应相合。宋代大儒张载言"为天地立心，为生民立命，为往圣继绝学，为万世开太平"，此传统文化精神之所在。有此精神，虽死犹生。若仅仅贪恋此身沉溺物欲，如庄子言"嗜欲深而天机浅"，此虽生犹死。

巍巍养生岂仅健身哉。

We conduct life nurturing practice not because we are scared of death and cravenly cling to life. Confucius once said, 'if you don't know life, how can you know death'? Only by living a life, can we thoroughly understand and follow the Dao between heaven and earth. Zhang Zai (1020–1077)[1] is most known for laying out four ontological goals for intellectuals: to build up the manifestations of Heaven and Earth's spirit, to build

---

1. A Chinese Neo-Confucian moral philosopher and cosmologist in the Song dynasty.

up good life for the public, to develop past sages' endangered scholarship, and to open up eternal peace for generation after generation. With this spirit, one can live even after death. However, for those with 'deep desires but shallow Heavenly sensitivities' (quotes from Zhuang Zi), their lives are already death.

# 意气君来骨肉臣

## Intention Acts as the King, Whereas Bones/Muscles are just Ministers

形，就是外在形体，皮毛肌肤，五脏六腑，简单说就是身。神，可以理解为人格精神、意志情感、思维方式，简单说就是心。此二者的关系犹如神（心）是主人，形（身）是屋舍。故在传统养生术中重神意而相对轻形质，拳论亦云"意气君来，骨肉臣"。

*Xing* means our body, including skin, muscle and internal organs, whereas *Shen* means our mind, including personality, willpower, emotions and mindset. Mind acts as the host and body as the house. In traditional qigong practice, intention acts as the King and bones/muscles are just ministers.

当今社会，一方面社会压力大，人如浮木，随波逐流。患病如抑郁、焦虑、亚健康等愈来愈多，患病年龄越来越轻。另一面社会信息量爆炸，声色犬马，夜生活多而至精神涣散，人的免疫力低下。《老子·十二章》"五色令人目盲，五音令人耳聋，五味令人口爽，驰骋畋猎令人心发狂，难得之货令人行妨。是以圣人为腹不为目，故去彼取此"。人在物欲世界追逐过多，迷失本性，故养生追求清新自然的生命活力——"生气"，往往是在人的命意源头——腰腹部丹田处才得以开启。而要开启这股力量必然要求我们的神意（心）合乎道，如《黄帝内经素问·上古天真论》"恬淡虚无，真气从之"。"恬淡虚无"便是道交感应的四种由浅入深的心灵境界；"真气"即"生气"。无此四种境界，"生气"无从谈起；一旦有此"生气"，五脏濡养，经络疏通，身形轻灵。

Stress in modern society can damage our health, causing depression, anxiety and physical imbalances. What's more, huge information, sensual pleasure and nightlife compromised our immune system. Chapter 12 of the Dao De Jing states, 'The five colors blind the eye. The five tones deafen the ear. The five flavors dull the taste. Racing and hunting madden the mind. Precious things lead one astray. Therefore the sage is guided by what he feels and not by what he sees. He lets go of that and chooses this'. Since one tends to be lost in excessive material desire, it's essential to pursue the natural vigor of life — vital qi in life nurturing exercise. The vital qi resides in the Dantian area. To activate vital qi, we need to guide our mental intent to the Dao. The genuine qi will be with us if we can achieve four levels of *Tian*, *Dan*, *Xu* and *Wu*. The 'genuine qi', i.e., the 'vital qi' can nourish internal organs, regulate meridians and help us stay healthy.

## 动 静 之 道
## Combination of Stillness and Motion

静，如老子言："致虚极，守静笃，万物并作，吾以观其复。夫物芸芸，各复归其根。归根曰静，静曰复命。" 不静不足与道相合。

As for stillness, the Dao De Jing states, 'Empty you of everything. Let the mind become still. The ten thousand things rise and fall while the Self watches their return. They grow and flourish and then return to the source. Returning to the source is stillness, which is the way of nature'.

动，如《吕祖百字铭》云：“真常须应物，应物要不迷。”不动不足以得道之灵通。

As for motion, the *Lü Zu Bai Zi Ming* (Hundred Words Stele by Lü Dongbin) says, 'the real ordinary mind should response to object sensed, but in responding should not get lost'.

动静之道，阴阳刚柔。一味死寂，全无变化，亦不是道，道性最活，变化无穷。浅显言之，《黄帝内经》云：“久视伤血，久卧伤气，久坐伤肉，久站伤骨，久行伤筋。”过静过动皆有妨碍。可见动静相宜，以静生动，以动养静，动静一如，才符合养生。

Active body movements need to be integrated into tranquil inner cultivation, just like the combination of yin softness and yang strength. According to the *Huang Di Nei Jing*, ' long-time use of your eyes damages your blood, long-time sitting damages your muscles, long-term standing damages your bones, long-time walking damages your tendons and long-time bed rest damages your qi'. Life can only be nurtured by balanced stillness and motion.

# 立 身 中 正

## Keep Your Body and Mind Upright

《黄帝内经》：“正气存内，邪不可干。”心正则身直，身直则脉顺，脉顺则气正，反之亦然。身心之间孕育浩然正气，外邪不可干扰。身正，才容易做到心正而气顺。初学者，没有比立身中正更重要的。简单地说，就是百会穴、会阴穴一线，体态中正安舒。气机发动，充盈后，再求变通。身形的姿态对气机发动有很好的辅助作用。身形包括五脏六腑、经络、四肢百骸，以及人生三宝之一的精。调身就是调整筋、膜、骨、肉等之间的相对运动及位置，使之符合练功中的气机的变化。练功过程中以神气运化为第一考量，骨肉随神气运化而改变，做到以意领形，以气催形。

The *Huang Di Nei Jing* states, 'when there is sufficient healthy qi inside, the pathogenic qi have no way to invade the body'. An upright mind leads to an upright body, which further leads to a smooth flow of qi and blood. When there is sufficient healthy qi in our body and mind, exogenous pathogens have no way to attack us. An upright body can help with concentration and free flow of qi. For beginners, it's extremely important to keep the body upright. Simply put, one needs to keep Baihui (DU 20)[1] and Huiyin (REN 1)[2] in the same line and stay comfortable. A good body posture can benefit qi activity. Regulating posture means to regulate internal organs, meridians, four limbs and essence (one of the three treasures). Regulating the body means to regulate the relative movements and locations of sinew, fascia, bones and muscles. The priority of qigong practice is to focus on mind and qi, followed by body movements. In other words, it is important to use intent to guide posture and use qi to adjust posture.

---

1. An acupuncture point located at the midpoint of the line connecting the apexes of the two auricles.
2. An acupuncture point located at the midpoint between the root of the scrotum and the anus in males, and at the midpoint between the posterior labial commissure and the anus in females.

八　段　锦　·　*Ba Duan Jin*

Movements of *Ba Duan Jin*

功法操作

# 基 础 操 作

## Basic posture

### 人字无极桩
### Stand in the *Wu Ji* position

人字无极桩示意图　Stand in the wuji position

［动作］两脚分开，距离同肩宽；两膝微曲，膝不过脚尖；两手自然下垂，双目垂帘。

[Description] Place your feet shoulder-width apart, slightly bend your knees (but do not let your knees extend past your toes), hang your arms loosely at your sides and keep your eyes half open and gaze down along the line of the nose.

[释义] 其核心为"抱元"。抱，混融也。元，即无极、元始、根本，即道。"道"，是产生万事万物的本源，是无形无象的一切"物质"的根本，是"天地万物之母"。一切有形的物质形态，一切无形的物质形态，都从"道"中分离出来的。此桩入手点在于入静，在于无我无为，清阳升而浊阴沉，不清而自清，浑然一体。

[Explanation] The essential concept of this posture is to *"Bao Yuan"*. The first word *'Bao'* means to mix with or to embrace. The second word *'Yuan'* means *Wu Ji* (nothingness), the primordial origin, the root or the *Dao*. The *'Dao'* is the spontaneous way that all things began, the foundation of all intangible and invisible 'substances' and activities, and the mother of all things in the universe. In summary, everything comes from the Dao. This standing posture requires a state of mindfulness, not-self and inaction, coupled with ascent of clean yang and descent of turbid yin.

## 抱球站桩
## Stand with imagination of holding a ball

[动作] 两脚分开，距离同肩宽；两膝微曲，膝不过脚尖；两手相抱于胸前。

[Description] Place your feet shoulder-width apart, slightly bend your knees and do not let your knees go past your toes, and then gently raise your arms until your hands are in front of your chest.

抱球站桩示意图　Stand with imagination of holding a ball

［释义］其势如抱一无形之球，其核心为"守一"。守，不离不弃也。一，太极也，阴阳未判之状态也。《道德经》云："天得一以清；地得一以宁；神得一以灵，谷得一以盈，万物得一以生，侯王得一以为天下正"。《太平经》云，"一者天之纲纪，万物之本也"，又云："夫一者，乃道之根也，气之始也"。《庄子》曰："至大无外，谓之大一，至小无内，谓之小一"。其特点在于动静如一，神气相依。外示安闲，内养精神。执先天一气之生机，融化后天浊气，气随神生，意随气转，气随神行，不离不弃，天人合一，与道合一。

[Explanation] This core of this posture is to 'Embrace the One'. Embrace here means never leave or given up. The one means Taiji, a state before separation of yin and yang. The *Dao De Jing* states, 'there were those in old times who grasped and were possessed of the One: The heaven was much clarified by attaining it. Likewise, the earth got stable or calm by the same [rotating] measure; and demon spirits or gods were spiritualized, became divine. The valley likewise became full, the abyss replenished. By staying in the one, all creatures lived and grew'. The *Tai Ping Jing*[1] (literally means Scripture on Great Peace) states, 'the One is the guiding principle of heaven and origin of all things', and 'the One is the root of Dao and beginning of qi'. The *Zhuang Zi* states, 'That which is so great that there is nothing outside it can be called the Great One; and that which is so small that there is nothing inside it can be called the Small One'. Characteristics of this posture: Integrated motion and stillness and mutual dependence of mind and qi. Externally, it looks relaxed. Internally, the mind is cultivated. Use the vitality of innate qi to melt down turbid postnatal qi. Use mental intent to guide qi and qi always flows with the mind. In the end, you are with the nature and Dao.

# 具 体 操 作

## Individual Movements

### 第一势　两手托天理三焦

#### Movement #1　Lift the Heavens with Two Hands to Regulate Sanjiao

[操作提示]该势主要是气机的升与降,使三焦气血阴降阳升。通过四肢和躯干的伸展运动,使手臂、颈、肩背、腰等部位的肌肉、骨骼、韧带得到调理,对颈椎病、肩周炎、腰背痛等有一定的防治作用。

---

1. Tai Ping Jing often refers to the work which has been preserved in the *Daozang*. It is considered to be a valuable resource for researching early Daoist beliefs and the society at the end of the Eastern Han dynasty.

[About this movement] This movement focuses on ascending and descending of qi in *Sanjiao*. It enables qi and yang to ascend and yin and blood to descend. Stretching of the four limbs and torso can regulate associated muscles, bones and ligaments and prevent or treat pain in the neck, shoulder and (low) back.

图1-1　Fig 1-1

抱球站桩：两脚分开，距离同肩宽；两膝微曲，膝不过脚尖；两手相抱于胸前。

Standing with imagination of holding a ball: Place your feet shoulder-width apart, slightly bend your knees and do not let your knees go past your toes, and raise your arms to the level of your chest.

双手从胸前沿身体两侧缓缓放下，合于小腹前。

Slowly drop the hands along both sides of the body and put two hands together in front of the lower abdomen.

图1-2　Fig 1-2

双手上提于胸前，略前送。

Lift the hands to the level of chest, slightly forward.

图1-3　Fig 1-3

双手上翻托于顶。

Turn the palms up and rise above the head.

图1-4　Fig 1-4

双手从顶部，两侧打开后合于胸前。

Open the hands from above the head to both side and close them in front of the chest.

图1-5　Fig 1-5

双手再次胸前打开。

Open the hands in front of the chest again.

图1-6　Fig 1-6

双手再次合于胸前。

Close the hands in front of the chest again.

图1-7　Fig 1-7

双手握拳合于小腹两侧。

Clench fists and close them on both sides of the lower abdomen.

图1-8　Fig 1-8

再次抱球站桩：两脚分开，距离同肩宽；两膝微曲，膝不过脚尖；两手相抱于胸前。

Return to standing posture with imagination of holding a ball: Place your feet shoulder-width apart, slightly bend your knees and do not let your knees go past your toes, and raise your arms to the level of your chest.

图1-9　Fig 1-9

# 第二势　左右开弓似射雕

## Movement #2　Draw the Bow both Left and Right-Handed to Shoot the Hawk

[操作提示]该势主要是气机的开与合。练习此势重点是膻中、神阙、气海开合从而增强心肺的功能，加强诸脏腑气血运行；通过伸臂、扩胸、转颈运动，使肩臂、颈部和胸肋部的肌肉、骨骼、韧带得到锻炼和加强。

[About this movement] This movement focuses on open and close of qi activity, especially on three points Danzhong (REN 17)[1], Shenque (REN 8)[2] and Qihai (REN 6)[3]. Arm extension, chest expansion and neck rotation strengthen muscles in the shoulder, arm, neck and rib-side area and benefit qi and blood circulation of the heart and lung.

抱球站桩：两脚分开、距离同肩宽；两膝微曲，膝不过脚尖；两手相抱于胸前。

Standing posture with imagination of holding a ball: Place your feet shoulder-width apart, slightly bend your knees and do not let your knees go past your toes, and raise your arms to the level of your chest.

图2-1　Fig 2-1

---

1. An acupuncture point located at the level with the 4th intercostal space, midway between the nipples.
2. An acupuncture point located at the center of the umbilicus.
3. An acupuncture point located 1.5 cun below the umbilicus.

身体右转、右脚尖点地，重心在左脚。双手胸前抱球。

Turn to the right side, touch the floor with the right tiptoe, and place the body weight on the left foot. Raise your arms to the level of your chest with imagination of holding a ball.

图2-2　Fig 2-2

右脚踩实，重心移至右脚，再将重心移至左脚，双手上提合于胸前，重心移至右脚。

Touch the floor with the right foot, shift the body weight to the left foot first and then to the right foot. Lift the hands and close them in front of the chest and shift the body weight to the right foot.

图2-3　Fig 2-3

重心再次后移至左脚，双手
从胸处前按，重心前移至右脚。

Shift the body weight to the left
foot again. Extend the hands forward
from the chest and shift the body
weight to the right foot.

图2-4　Fig 2-4

重心移至右脚，左旋180°。左
手向下划弧线，从身体左侧前伸。

Shift the body weight to the
right foot, turn 180° to the left. Draw
a downward arc using the left hand
and extend forward from left side of
the body.

图2-5　Fig 2-5

双手从身体两侧向下划弧线，交叉合于胸前。

Draw downward arcs using both hands and cross the hands in front of the chest.

图2-6　Fig 2-6

双手握拳合于小腹两侧。

Clench fists and close them on both sides of the lower abdomen.

图2-7　Fig 2-7

再次抱球站桩：两脚分开、距离同肩宽；两膝微曲，膝不过脚尖；两手相抱于胸前。

Return to standing posture with imagination of holding a ball. Place your feet shoulder-width apart, slightly bend your knees and do not let your knees go past your toes, and raise your arms to the level of your chest.

图2-8　Fig 2-8

身体左转，左脚尖点地，重心在右脚。双手胸前抱球。

Turn to the left, touch the floor with the left tiptoe and place the body weight on the right foot. Raise your arms to the level of your chest with imagination of holding a ball.

图2-9　Fig 2-9

左脚踩实，重心移至左脚，再将重心移至右脚，双手上提合于胸前。

Touch the floor with the left foot, shift the body weight to the Left foot first and then to the right foot. Lift the hands and close them in front of the chest.

图2-10　Fig 2-10

重心再次后移至右脚，双手从胸处前按，重心前移至左脚。

Shift the body weight to the right foot extend the hands forward from the chest and shift the body weight to the left foot.

图2-11　Fig 2-11

重心移至左脚，右旋180°。右手向下划弧线，从身体右侧前伸。

Shift the body weight to the left foot, turn 180° to the right. Draw a downward arc using the right hand and extend forward from right side of the body.

图2-12　Fig 2-12

双手从身体两侧向下划弧线，交叉合于胸前。

Draw downward arcs using both hands and cross the hands in front of the chest.

图2-13　Fig 2-13

双手握拳合于小腹两侧。

Clench fists and put them on both sides of the lower abdomen.

图2-14　Fig 2-14

抱球站桩：两脚分开，距离同肩宽；两膝微曲，膝不过脚尖；两手相抱于胸前。

Return to standing posture with imagination of holding a ball: Place your feet shoulder-width apart, slightly bend your knees and do not let your knees go past your toes, and raise your arms to the level of your chest.

图2-15　Fig 2-15

## 第三势　调理脾胃须单举

[操作提示]该势主要是气机的一升一降,形成气机的左旋与右旋。此势主要作用在上下旋转争力,使两侧的肌肉和肝胆脾胃等脏器受到牵引,促进胃肠的蠕动,改善消化功能。

[About the movement] This movement focuses on ascending, descending and left/right rotation of qi activity. By upward and downward rotation, this movement can influence muscles on both sides and internal organs including the liver, gallbladder, spleen and stomach, thus increasing the gastrointestinal peristalsis and improving digestion.

图3-1　Fig 3-1

抱球站桩:两脚分开,距离同肩宽;两膝微曲,膝不过脚尖;两手相抱于胸前。

Standing posture with imagination of holding a ball: Place your feet shoulder-width apart, slightly bend your knees and do not let your knees go past your toes, and raise your arms to the level of your chest.

转化成竖抱球站桩，右手在下，重心在左脚。

Shift to standing posture with imagination of holding a ball longitudinally, with left hand on top and right hand down. Place the body weight on the left foot.

图3-2　Fig 3-2

双手交叉转换，做3次，由小至大。

Cross the hands, repeat 3 times and gradually increase the ball in imagination.

图3-3　Fig 3-3

右手上托，左手下按。

Lift the right hand, press the left hand down.

图3-4　Fig 3-4

抱球站桩：两脚分开，距离同肩宽；两膝微曲，膝不过脚尖；两手相抱于胸前。

Return to standing posture with imagination of holding a ball: Place your feet shoulder-width apart, slightly bend your knees and do not let your knees go past your toes, and raise your arms to the level of your chest.

图3-5　Fig 3-5

转化成竖抱球站桩，左手在下，重心偏右脚。

Shift to standing posture with imagination of holding a ball longitudinally, with right hand on top and left hand down. Place the body weight on the right foot.

图3-6　Fig 3-6

双手交叉转换，做3次，由小至大。

Cross hands, repeat 3 times and gradually increase the ball in imagination.

图3-7　Fig 3-7

左手上托，右手下按。

Lift the left hand, press the right hand down.

图3-8　Fig 3-8

抱球站桩：两脚分开、距离同肩宽；两膝微曲，膝不过脚尖；两手相抱于胸前。

Return to standing posture with imagination of holding a ball: Place your feet shoulder-width apart, slightly bend your knees and do not let your knees go past your toes, and raise your arms to the level of your chest.

图3-9　Fig 3-9

# 第四势　五劳七伤往后瞧

Movement #4　Look from Side to Side to Prevent Five Overstrains and Seven Injuries

[操作提示]该势主要是气机的螺旋圆运动。此势能使整个脊柱、两大腿，乃至全身均得到运动，有助于改善神经系统功能，消除疲劳，从而使脏腑气血得以调整。可用于防治高血压、颈椎病、眼病。

[About the movement] This movement focuses on spiral circling of qi activity. By working on the spine and thighs, it helps to regulate functions of the nervous system, improve fatigue and harmonize qi and blood. This movement also helps to prevent and treat hypertension, cervical spondylosis and eye problems.

图4-1　Fig 4-1

抱球站桩，两脚分开，距离同肩宽；两膝微曲，膝不过脚尖；两手相抱于胸前。

Standing posture with imagination of holding a ball: Place your feet shoulder-width apart, slightly bend your knees and do not let your knees go past your toes, and raise your arms to the level of your chest.

右脚向后45°移动，双手身前
翻动如滚球。

Move the right foot 45° backward
and turn the hands like rolling a ball.

图4-2　Fig 4-2

身体右后旋转，带动双手上
举如抱球。

Turn the body to the right and
back, move the hands like holding a
ball.

图4-3　Fig 4-3

身体下蹲左旋，带动双手下捧如抱球。

Squat down and turn left, move the hands like holding a ball.

图4-4　Fig 4-4

身体继续左旋直至左脚后侧，带动双手下捧如抱球。

Continue to turn the body to the left until the back of the left foot. Move the hands like holding a ball.

图4-5　Fig 4-5

身体转正，带动双手上举如
抱球。

Turn the body upright and lift the
hands like holding a ball.

图4-6　　Fig 4-6

双手缓缓下移如抱球下按。

Slowly drop the hands like holding
a ball.

图4-7　　Fig 4-7

图4-8　Fig 4-8

　　身体重心左移，左脚向右移动，双手打开，右手下移至右腿旁侧。右手再沿右腿旁侧下移，身体重心右移。

Shift the body weight to the left side, move the left foot to right, open the hands and drop the right hand to the lateral side of the right leg. Drop the right hand along the lateral side of the right leg, shift the body weight to the right side.

图4-9　Fig 4-9

　　身体重心移至右脚，右手上托。

Shift the body weight to the right foot and lift the right hand.

图4-10　Fig 4-10

身体左旋，左手沿左腿旁侧下移，重心左移。

Turn the body to left, drop the left hand along the lateral side of the left leg and shift the body weight to the left side.

图4-11　Fig 4-11

身体重心移至左脚，左手上托。

Shift the body weight to the left foot and lift the left hand.

抱球站桩，两脚分开，距离同肩宽；两膝微曲、膝不过脚尖；两手相抱于胸前。

Return to standing posture with imagination of holding a ball: Place your feet shoulder-width apart, slightly bend your knees and do not let your knees go past your toes, and raise your arms to the level of your chest.

图4-12　Fig 4-12

左脚向后45°移动，双手身前翻动如滚球。

Move the left foot 45° backward and turn the hands like rolling a ball.

图4-13　Fig 4-13

身体右后旋转，带动双手上
举如抱球。

Turn the body to right and back,
lift the hands like holding a ball.

图4-14　Fig 4-14

身体下蹲左旋，带动双手下
捧如抱球。

Squat down and turn left, move
the hands like holding a ball.

图4-15　Fig 4-15

身体继续左旋直至左脚后侧,带动双手下捧如抱球。

Continue turning the body to left until the back of the left foot and move the hands like holding a ball.

图4-16　Fig 4-16

身体转正,带动双手上举如抱球。

Turn the body upright and lift the hands like holding a ball.

图4-17　Fig 4-17

双手缓缓下移如抱球。

Slowly drop the hands like holding a ball.

图4-18　　Fig 4-18

身体重心右移，右脚向左移动，双手打开，左手下移至左腿旁侧。左手再沿左腿旁侧下移，身体重心左移。

Shift the body weight to the right side, move the right foot to the left, open the hands and then place the left hand down to the lateral side of the left leg. Drop the left hand along the lateral side of the left leg and shift the body weight to the left side.

图4-19　　Fig 4-19

身体重心移至左脚，左手上托。

Shift the body weight to the left
foot and lift the left hand.

图4-20  Fig 4-20

身体右旋，右手沿左腿旁侧下
移，重心右移。

Turn to the right, drop the right
hand along the lateral side of the
right leg and shift the body weight to
the right side.

图4-21  Fig 4-21

身体重心移至右脚，右手上托。

Shift the body weight to the right foot and lift the right hand.

图4-22　Fig 4-22

抱球站桩，两脚分开、距离同肩宽；两膝微曲，膝不过脚尖；两手相抱于胸前。

Return to standing posture with imagination of holding a ball: Place your feet shoulder-width apart, slightly bend your knees and do not let your knees go past your toes, and raise your arms to the level of your chest.

图4-23　Fig 4-23

*Ba Duan Jin* · 八 段 锦 · 功 法 操 作 · *Movements of Ba Duan Jin*

# 第五势　摇头摆尾去心火

## Movement #5　Sway the Head and Shake to Clear Heart-Fire

［操作提示］该势主要是气沉丹田，敛气入骨。练习此式势强调入静放松，"虚其心实其腹"，使心肾相交。同时运动腰、颈部的关节，有助于任、督、冲三脉经气的运行。可用于防治颈椎、腰椎疾病，以及心火亢盛所致的失眠、心烦、心悸等症。

[About the movement] This movement focuses on qi sinking down to Dantian and restrain qi within bones. By exercising lumbar and cervical joints, this movement can regulate qi circulation in Ren, Du and Chong meridians and harmonize heart fire and kidney water. It can also prevent or treat neck back, low back pain and problems due to heart-fire hyperactivity such as insomnia, restlessness and palpitations.

抱球站桩，两脚分开，距离同肩宽；两膝微曲、膝不过脚尖；两手相抱于胸前。

Standing posture with imagination of holding a ball: Place your feet shoulder-width apart, slightly bend your knees and do not let your knees go past your toes, and raise your arms to the level of your chest.

图5-1　Fig 5-1

运气如球带动身体右旋，身形缓缓向下。

Move qi like moving the imaginary ball to turn the body to right, slightly squat down.

图5-2　Fig 5-2

运气如球带动身体左旋，身形缓缓向下。

Move qi like moving the imaginary ball to turn the body to left, slightly squat down.

图5-3　Fig 5-3

运气如球带动身体右旋，身形缓缓向下。

Move qi like moving the imaginary ball to turn the body to right, slightly squat down.

图5-4　Fig 5-4

运气如球带动身体左旋，身形缓缓向下。

Move qi like moving the imaginary ball to turn the body to left, slightly squat down.

图5-5　Fig 5-5

运气如球带动身体右旋，身形缓缓向下。

Move qi like moving the imaginary ball to turn the body to right, slightly squat down.

图5-6　Fig 5-6

运气如球带动身体右旋，身形缓缓向上。

Move qi like moving the imaginary ball, slowly lift the body.

图5-7　Fig 5-7

抱球站桩，两脚分开，距离同
肩宽；两膝微曲，膝不过脚尖；两
手相抱于胸前。

Return to standing posture with
imagination of holding a ball: Place
your feet shoulder-width apart,
slightly bend your knees and do not
let your knees go past your toes, and
raise your arms to the level of your
chest.

图5-8　Fig 5-8

运气如球带动身体左旋，身
形缓缓向下。

Move qi like moving the imaginary
ball to turn the body to left, slowing
squat down.

图5-9　Fig 5-9

运气如球带动身体右旋，身形缓缓向下。

Move qi like moving the imaginary ball to turn the body to right, slowly tilt the body.

图5-10　Fig 5-10

运气如球带动身体左旋，身形缓缓向下。

Move qi like moving the imaginary ball to turn the body to left, slowly squat down.

图5-11　Fig 5-11

运气如球带动身体右旋，身形缓缓向下。

Move qi like moving the imaginary ball to turn the body to right, slowly squat down.

图5-12　Fig 5-12

运气如球带动身体右旋，身形缓缓向下。

Move qi like moving the imaginary ball to turn the body to left, slowly squat down.

图5-13　Fig 5-13

运气如球带动身体右旋，身形缓缓向上。

Move qi like moving the imaginary ball to turn the body to right, slowly lift the body.

图5-14　Fig 5-14

抱球站桩，两脚分开、距离同肩宽；两膝微曲，膝不过脚尖；两手相抱于胸前。

Return to standing posture with imagination of holding a ball. Place your feet shoulder-width apart, slightly bend your knees and do not let your knees go past your toes, and raise your arms to the level of your chest.

图5-15　Fig 5-15

## 第六势　两手攀足固肾腰

［操作提示］该势主要是壮命门之真火。重点在腰部，腰为肾之府，长期运动腰部可起到和带脉，通任督的作用。具有强肾、醒脑、明目的功效。

[About the movement] This movement focuses on strengthening the real fire of the vital gate in the lumbus (known as the house of kidney). It can regulate Dai, Ren and Du meridians, benefit the kidney, refresh mind and improve the eyesight.

图6-1　Fig 6-1

抱球站桩，两脚分开，距离同肩宽；两膝微曲，膝不过脚尖；两手相抱于胸前。

Standing posture with imagination of holding a ball: Place your feet shoulder-width apart, slightly bend your knees and do not let your knees go past your toes, and raise your arms to the level of your chest.

双手上托如捧球状，腰部略
弯如含球状。

Lift the hands and bend the
waist area liking holding a ball.

图6-2　Fig 6-2

下腰，双手下按于脚背，全身
如伏按一球上。

Bend the waist area and press the
hands down like pressing a ball.

图6-3　Fig 6-3

运气如球，轻托腰部升起。

Move qi like moving a ball and gently lift the waist area.

图6-4　Fig 6-4

运气如球，沉入脚底，腰部缓缓落下。

Move qi like moving a ball to the soles. Slowly drop the waist area.

图6-5　Fig 6-5

运气如球，轻托腰部，人缓缓升起。

Move qi like moving a ball, gently support the low back and slowly lift the body.

图6-6    Fig 6-6

抱球站桩，两脚分开、距离同肩宽；两膝微曲、膝不过脚尖；两手相抱于胸前。

Return to standing posture with imagination of holding a ball: Place your feet shoulder-width apart, slightly bend your knees and do not let your knees go past your toes, and raise your arms to the level of your chest.

图6-7    Fig 6-7

## 第七势 攒拳怒目增气力
## Movement #7　Clench the Fists and Glare Angrily to Increase Strength

[操作提示]该势主要是神机灌顶,目露精光;气沉丹田,沉胯圆裆。该势主要运动四肢、腰和眼肌,能增强肺气,增加肌力。具有强筋健骨之功。

[About the movement] This movement focuses on qi reaching the vertex, qi sinking down to Dantian and opening up and relaxing the hip joints. By excising muscles of the four limbs, low back and eyes, this movement can supplement lung qi, increase muscle strength and benefit sinews and bones.

图7-1　Fig 7-1

抱球站桩,两脚分开,距离同肩宽;两膝微曲,膝不过脚尖;两手相抱于胸前。

Standing posture with imagination of holding a ball: Place your feet shoulder-width apart, slightly bend your knees and do not let your knees go past your toes, and raise your arms to the level of your chest.

运气如球右旋，身体重心在左脚，轻提右脚尖。抱球向右45°。

Move qi like moving a ball to turn the body to right, place the body weight on the left foot, gently lift the right tiptoe and turn 45° to right with the imagination of holding a ball.

图7-2　Fig 7-2

运气如球，向下，向右前45°滚动，带动身体重心右前45°移至右脚，双手向前捧球。

Move qi like moving a ball and turn 45° right and downward. Shift the body weight 45° forward to the right foot and hold the ball forward in the hands.

图7-3　Fig 7-3

运气如球，内下旋转，带动身体重心移至左脚，双手身形作伏按球状。

Move qi like moving a ball and turn inward and downward to shift the body weight to the left foot. Then use the hands to press the ball.

图7-4　Fig 7-4

运气如球，向上向前45°，迅速带动身体重心移至右脚，双手握拳击出。

Move qi like moving a ball 45° upward and forward to shift the body weight to the right foot. Then punch with the fists.

图7-5　Fig 7-5

抱球站桩、两脚分开、距离同肩宽；两膝微曲、膝不过脚尖；两手相抱于胸前。

Return to standing posture with imagination of holding a ball. Place your feet shoulder-width apart, slightly bend your knees and do not let your knees go past your toes, and raise your arms to the level of your chest.

图7-6　Fig 7-6

运气如球左旋、身体重心在右脚、轻提左脚尖。抱球向左45°。

Move qi like moving a ball, turn to left, place the body weight on the right foot and lift the left tiptoe. Hold the imaginary ball in the hands and turn 45° to the left side.

图7-7　Fig 7-7

*Ba Duan Jin* · 八段锦

功法操作 · *Movements of Ba Duan Jin*

运气如球，向下，向左前45°
滚动，带动身体重心向左前45°移
至左脚，双手向前捧球。

Move qi like moving a ball
downward. Roll the ball 45° forward
to shift the body weight 45° left and
forward to the left foot. Hold the ball
in the hands.

图7-8    Fig 7-8

运气如球，内下旋转，带动身
体重心移至右脚，双手身形作伏
按球状。

Move qi like moving a ball, turn
inward and downward to shift the
body weight to the right foot. Use the
hands to press the imaginary ball.

图7-9    Fig 7-9

运气如球，向上向前45°，迅速带动身体重心移至左脚，双手握拳击出。

Move qi like moving a ball 45° upward and forward to shift the body weight to the left foot. Then punch with the fists.

图7-10    Fig 7-10

抱球站桩，两脚分开，距离同肩宽；两膝微曲，膝不过脚尖；两手相抱于胸前。

Return to standing posture with imagination of holding a ball. Place your feet shoulder-width apart, slightly bend your knees and do not let your knees go past your toes, and raise your arms to the level of your chest.

图7-11    Fig 7-11

## 第八势 背后七颠百病消
## Movement #8 7 Times of Bouncing to Relieve All Diseases

[操作提示] 该势主要是神意向上，气机向下，顶天立地之势。两脚跟有节律的弹性起落，通过震动，使椎骨之间各关节韧带得以锻炼，并使浊气自涌泉排出；同时有利于脑脊液的循环和脊髓神经功能的增强，防治椎体病变。

[About the movement] This movement focuses on ascending of mental intent and descending of qi activity. Rhythmic bouncing of the feet can benefit intervertebral joints and ligaments and help to remove turbid qi from Yongquan (KI 1)[1]. This movement can benefit circulation of cerebrospinal fluid and spinal cord and thus prevent or treat vertebral disorders.

抱球站桩，两脚分开，距离同肩宽；两膝微曲，膝不过脚尖；两手相抱于胸前。

Standing posture with imagination of holding a ball: Place your feet shoulder-width apart, slightly bend your knees and do not let your knees go past your toes, and raise your arms to the level of your chest.

图8-1 Fig 8-1

---

1. An acupuncture point located on the sole, in the depression appearing on the anterior part of the sole when the foot is in the plantar flexion, approximately at the junction of the anterior third and posterior two thirds of the line connecting the base of the 2nd and 3rd toes and the heel.

运气如球，轻落入脚底，带
动身体重心及双手缓缓落下。

Move qi like moving a ball to the
soles to shift the body weight. Slowly
drop the hands.

图8-2　Fig 8-2

运气如球，阴降阳升，身体重
心下沉，双手轻提至命门处。

Move qi like moving a ball to
allow yin to descend and yang to
ascend. Sink the body weight and
gently lift the hands to Mingmen¹
area.

图8-3　Fig 8-3

1. Ming Men literally means the gate of life, located between the kidneys, at the level of
the second lumbar vertebrae.

运气如球，阴降阳升，带动身体双脚迅速跳动，双手迅速落下。图8-3、图8-4再重复6次。

Move qi like moving a ball to allow yin to descend and yang to ascend. Follow this with fast bouncing of the feet and dropping of the hands. Then repeat 8.3 and 8.4 6 times.

图8-4　Fig 8-4

抱球站桩、两脚分开、距离同肩宽；两膝微曲，膝不过脚尖；两手相抱于胸前。

Return to standing posture with imagination of holding a ball: Place your feet shoulder-width apart, slightly bend your knees and do not let your knees go past your toes, and raise your arms to the level of your chest.

图8-5　Fig 8-5

八 段 锦 · *Ba Duan Jin*

Application

应用

# 整 体 调 整
## Multidirectional Regulation

八段锦由静而松，由松而活，由活而气血融通，内外如一。八段锦，道家用以变化气质，脱胎换骨以救静坐气滞血枯之弊；习武用以易筋展脉，气运周身；养生则用以祛病延年，修身养性。八段锦重视整体调整，重点在"神，气"盈虚开合。以《黄帝内经》"正气存内，邪不可干"、"恬淡虚无，真气从之"为宗旨。关注人的所有方面，从更本质的角度看，练功改变的是生活态度、方式，使生命焕发出新的能量、新的状态。旧去新来之间，如《庄子·齐物论》"方生方死，方死方生；方可方不可，方不可方可"来体悟生命之妙。

Ba Duan Jin movements help us to achieve tranquility first, then relaxation, and finally smooth circulation of qi and blood. Taoists practice Ba Duan Jin to resolve qi stagnation and blood stasis due to long-term meditation. Martial artists practice Ba Duan Jin to stretch the sinews and move qi throughout the entire body. Health cultivation advocates practice Ba Duan Jin to remove diseases, achieve longevity and cultivate one's moral character. Ba Duan Jin can regulate our body and mind in a comprehensive way. It is strongly based on the theory that 'when there is sufficient healthy qi inside, the pathogenic qi have no way to invade the body' and 'genuine qi will be with you when you achieve Tian (peaceful joy), Dan (no greed for fame and wealth), Xu (void) and Wu (nothingness)'. Actually, Ba Duan Jin practice can change our life attitude and lifestyle and rekindle new energy to experience the subtle beauty of life, just

# 疾 病 的 防 治

## Disease Prevention and Treatment

　　练功若到时时"恬淡之心,处无为之事",自然"正气存内,邪不可干","精神内守 病安从来"。只可惜身处红尘空华,名利所累,儿女情长,不在病中,便在烦恼中。若做不到"时时",但求"有时",甚或"一时""恬淡之心",配合八段锦导引,辅以特殊发音呼吸可针对不同病患进行辨证施功。如肝郁气滞,表现为胸闷,急躁易怒,两胁胀痛,头晕耳鸣等,当疏肝理气,可选练第一、第二势。脾虚气滞,表现为脘腹胀痛,食少纳呆,恶心呕吐,消化不良等,应健脾理气,可用第二、第三势。心肾不交,眩晕耳鸣,失眠多梦,腰膝酸软,五心烦热,当交通心肾,补肾清心,可用第五、第六势。清阳不升,可用第四、第七势;肝阳上亢,可用第四、第八势。心脑血管病者,选练前四势为宜;呼吸系统疾病者,多练第一、第二、第三、第七势;消化系统疾病,多练第三、第五势;颈腰椎病者,多练第四、第五、第六势等。以上种种又当参考阴阳虚实,表里寒热,气息盈亏,因人、因时、因地而作不同变化。

If we are equipped with a peaceful mind and sufficient healthy qi, we won't get sick. However, it's unlikely to be free from worries in the real world. Occasional peaceful joy, Ba Duan Jin and healing sounds can help us to address different health problems. Examples are as follows:

For liver-qi stagnation manifesting as chest tightness, irritability, distending pain in the rib-side area, dizziness and tinnitus, practice #1 and #2 movements on a regular basis.

For spleen deficiency and qi stagnation manifesting as abdominal distension and pain, a poor appetite, nausea, vomiting and indigestion, it's advisable to practice # 2 and # 3 movements.

For disharmony between the heart and kidney manifesting as dizziness, tinnitus, insomnia, dream-disturbed sleep, soreness and weakness in the low back and knee joints, feverish sensations in the palms, soles and chest, practice # 5 and # 6 movements.

For failure of clean yang to ascend, practice # 4 and # 7 movements.

For hyperactivity of liver-yang, practice # 4 and # 8 movements.

For cerebro-cardiovascular diseases, practice the first four movements.

For respiratory system conditions, practice # 1, # 2, # 3 and # 7 movements.

For digestive system problems, practice # 3 and # 5 movements.

For neck and low back pain, practice # 4, # 5 and # 6 movements.

It's worth noting that many factors need to be taken into consideration. These may include yin, yang, deficiency, excess, exterior, interior, cold, heat, individualized constitution, geographical locations and seasons.

八 段 锦 • *Ba Duan Jin*

The Meridian Charts

经络图

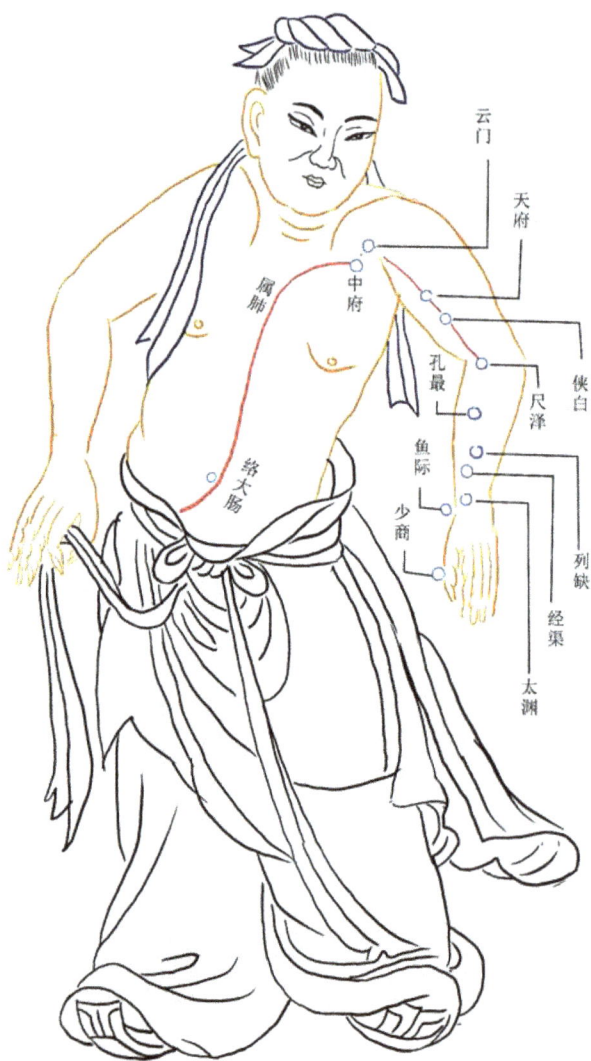

云门

天府

中府

属肺

侠白

尺泽

孔最

鱼际

络大肠

少商

列缺

经渠

太渊

## 手太阴肺经

Lung Meridian of Hand-Taiyin

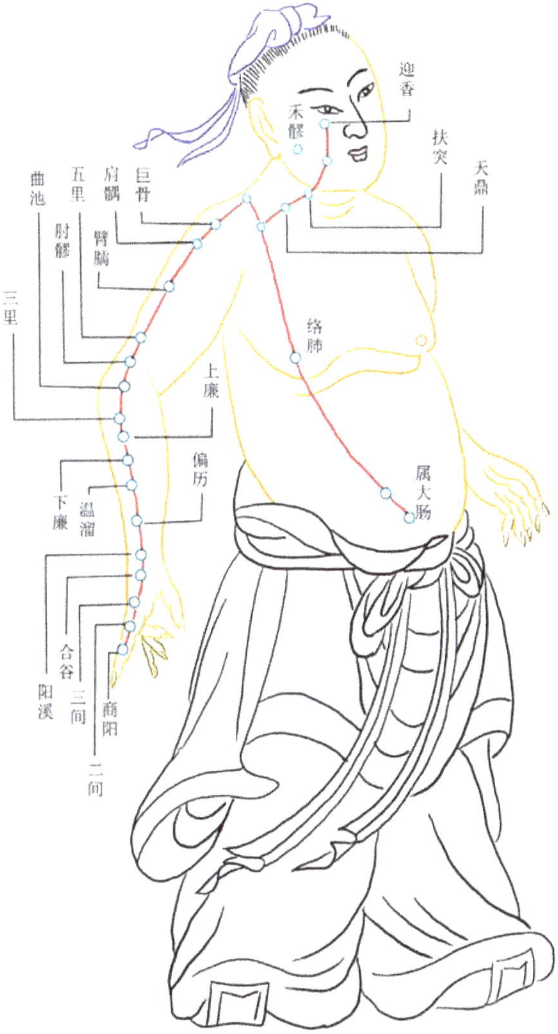

迎香
禾髎
扶突
天鼎
巨骨
肩髃
臂臑
曲池
五里
肘髎
三里
络肺
上廉
偏历
属大肠
下廉
温溜
合谷
阳溪
三间
二间
商阳

# 手阳明大肠经

Large Intestine Meridian of Hand-Yangming

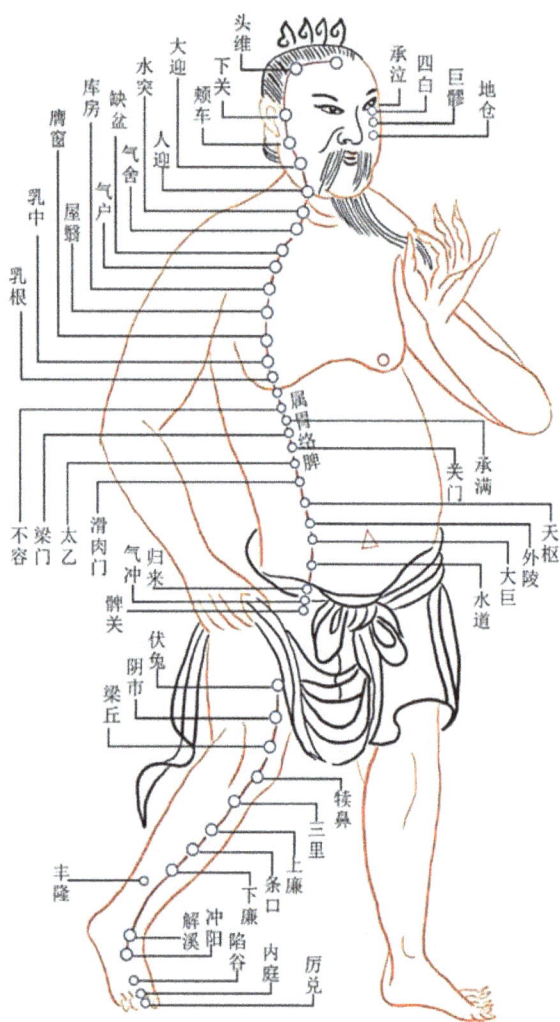

足阳明胃经

Stomach Meridian of Foot-Yangming

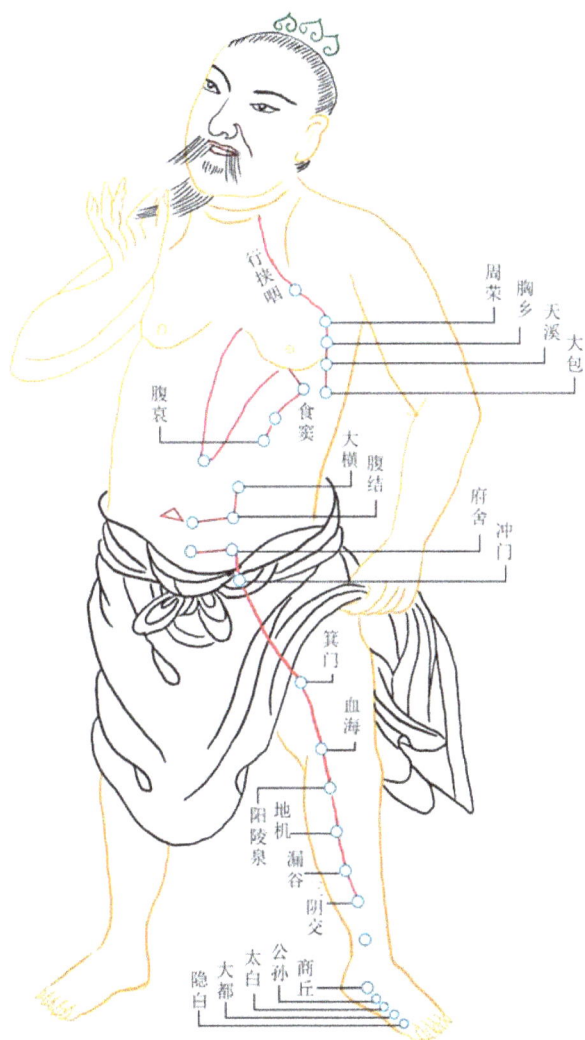

足太阴脾经

Spleen Meridian of Foot-Taiyin

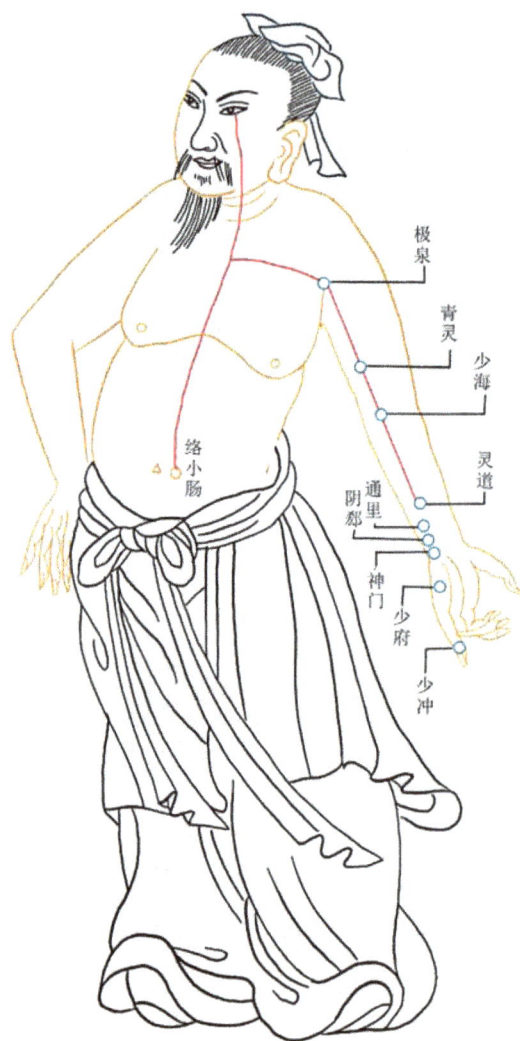

极泉

青灵

少海

灵道

络小肠

通里

阴郄

神门

少府

少冲

## 手少阴心经

Heart Meridian of Hand-Shaoyin

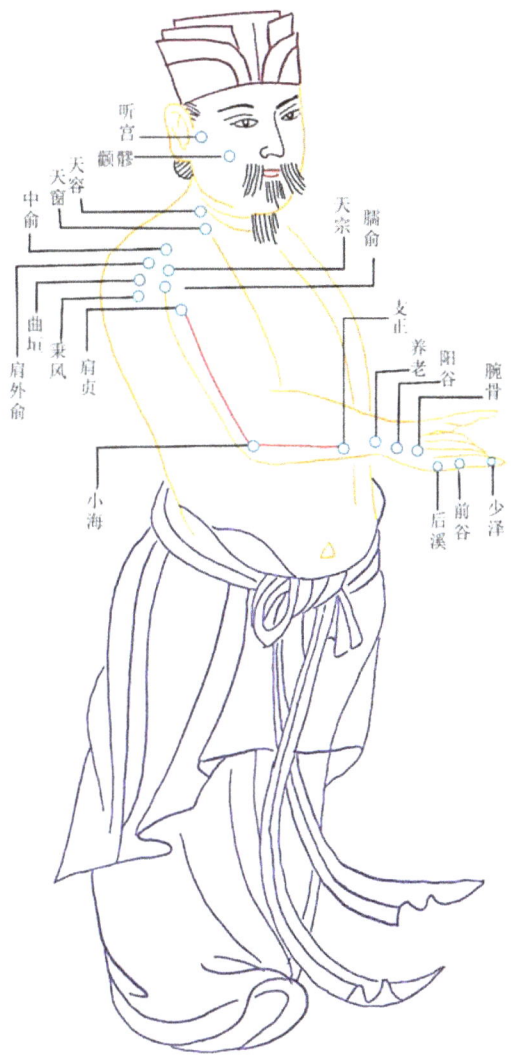

# 手太阳小肠经

Small Intestine Meridian of Hand-Taiyang

承光 五处 曲差 攒竹 睛明

玉枕 络却 通天

天柱

大杼 风门 肺俞 厥阴俞 心俞 膈俞

肝俞

胆俞

附分

魄户 膏肓 神堂 譩譆 膈关 阳纲

意舍 魂门

脾俞 胃俞 肾俞 三焦俞

肓门 志室 胞肓

胃仓

秩边

承扶

会阳 白环俞 中膂俞 膀胱俞 小肠俞 大肠俞

浮郄

委阳

殷门

委中 合阳

承筋 承山 络飞阳 跗阳

昆仑 仆参 申脉 金门 京骨 束骨 通谷 至阴

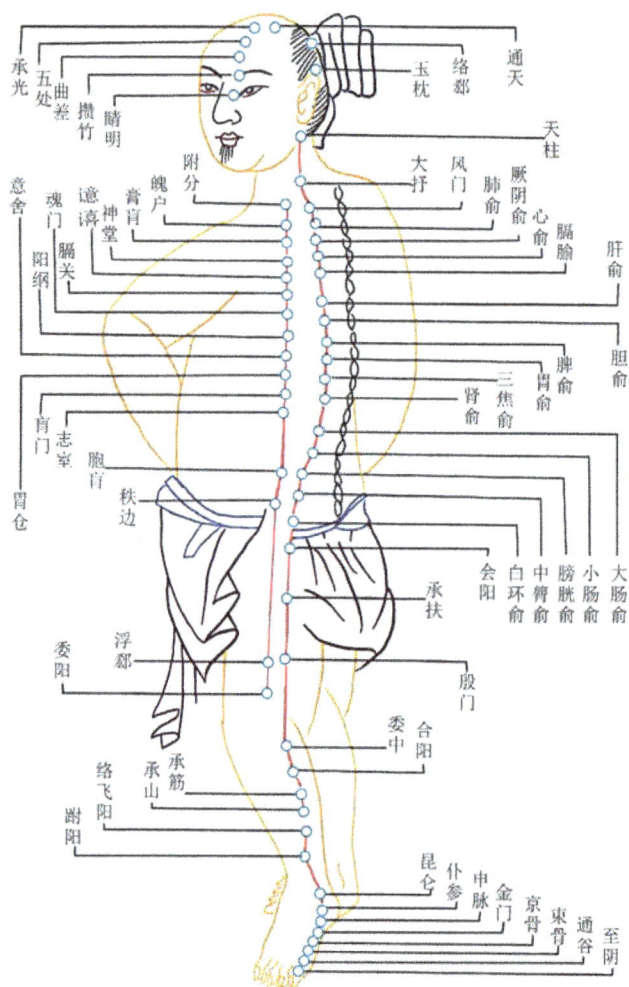

# 足太阳膀胱经

Bladder Meridian of Foot-Taiyang

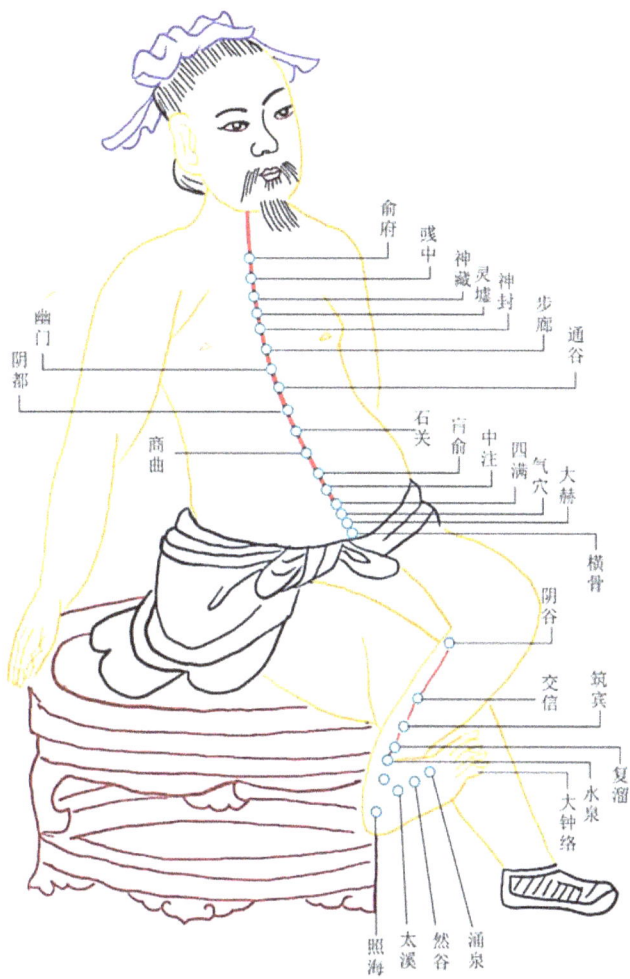

俞府
彧中
神藏
灵墟
神封
步廊
通谷
幽门
阴都
石关
商曲
腹通谷
中注
四满
气穴
大赫
横骨
阴谷
交信
筑宾
复溜
水泉
大钟络
照海
太溪
然谷
涌泉

足少阴肾经

Kidney Meridian of Foot-Shaoyin

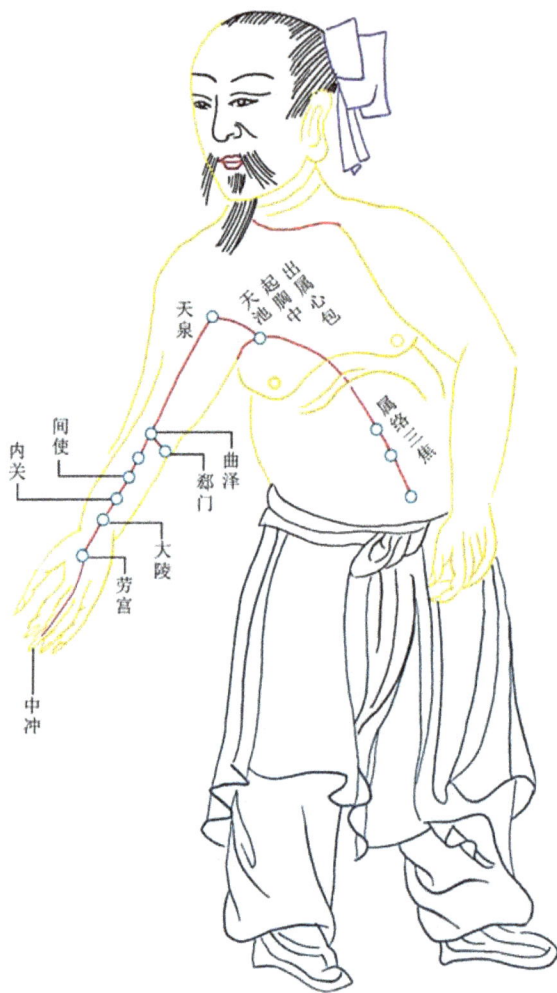

手厥阴心包经

Pericardium Meridian of Hand-Jueyin

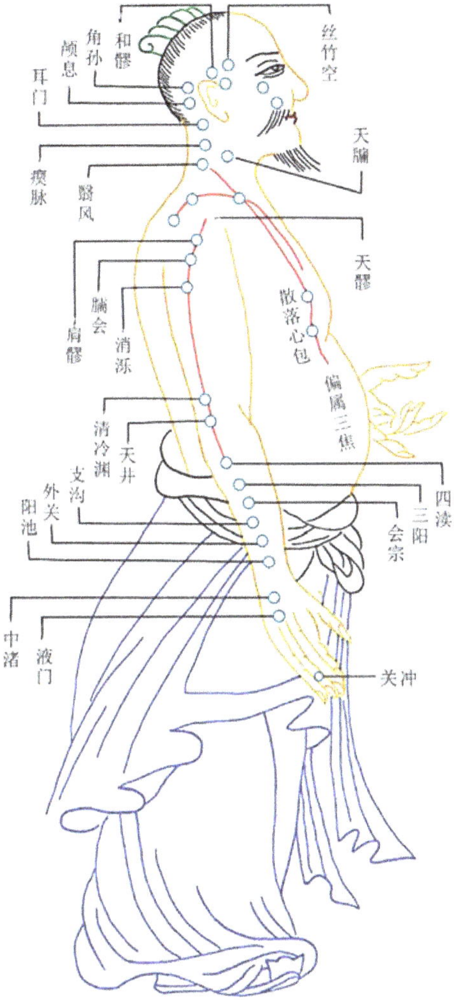

絲竹空
和髎
角孫
颅息
耳门
天牖
瘈脉
翳风
天髎
臑会
肩髎
消泺
散落心包
清冷渊
天井
偏属三焦
支沟
外关
阳池
四渎
三阳
会宗
中渚
液门
关冲

手少阳三焦经

Triple Energizer Meridian of Hand-Shaoyang

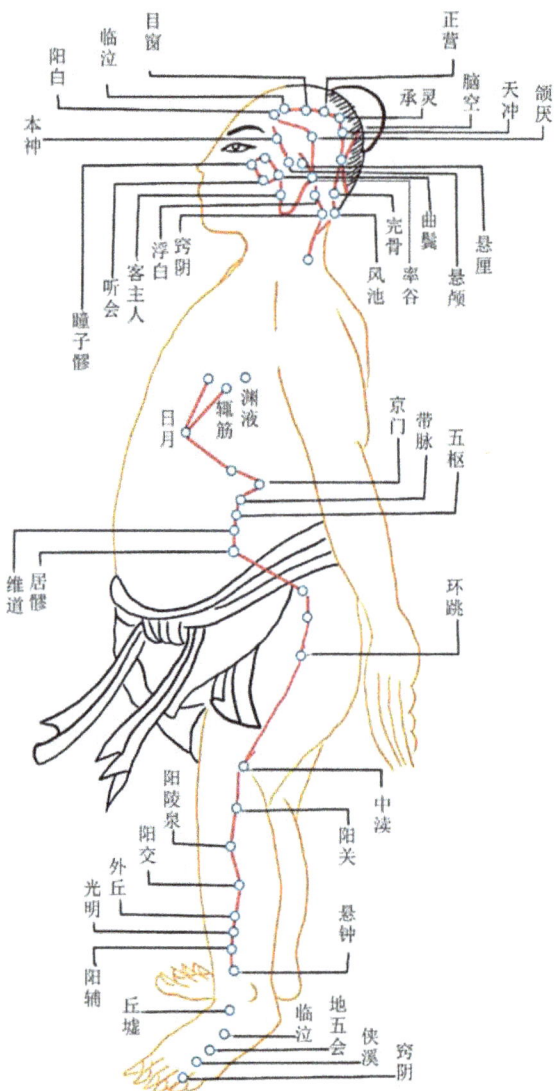

足少阳胆经

Gallbladder Meridian of Foot-Shaoyang

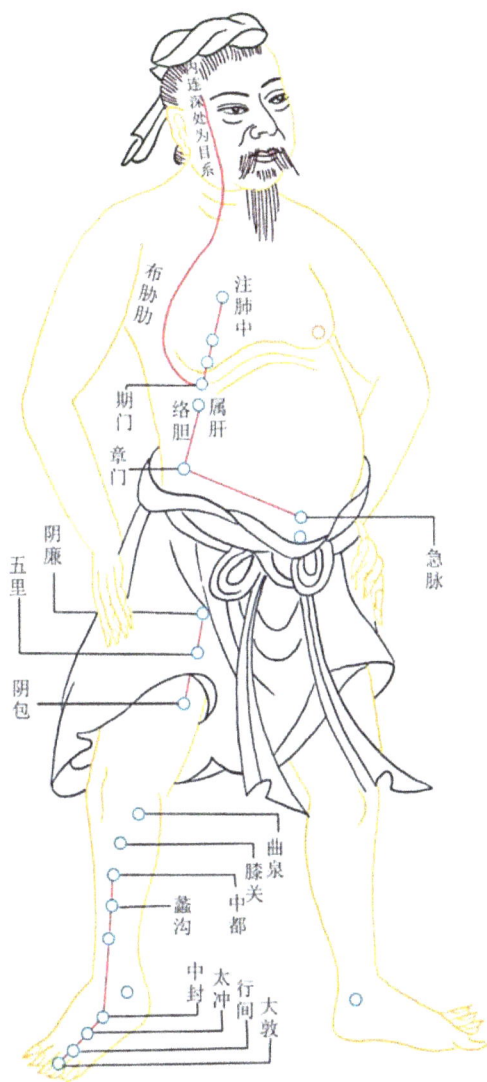

足厥阴肝经

Liver Meridian of Foot-Jueyin

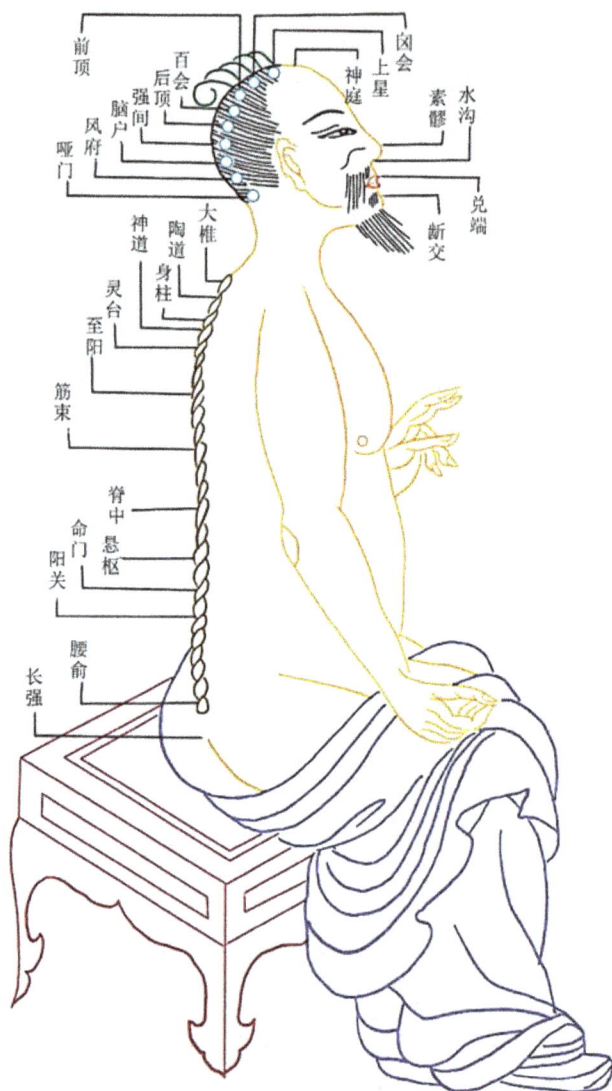

督脉

Governor Vessel (Du)

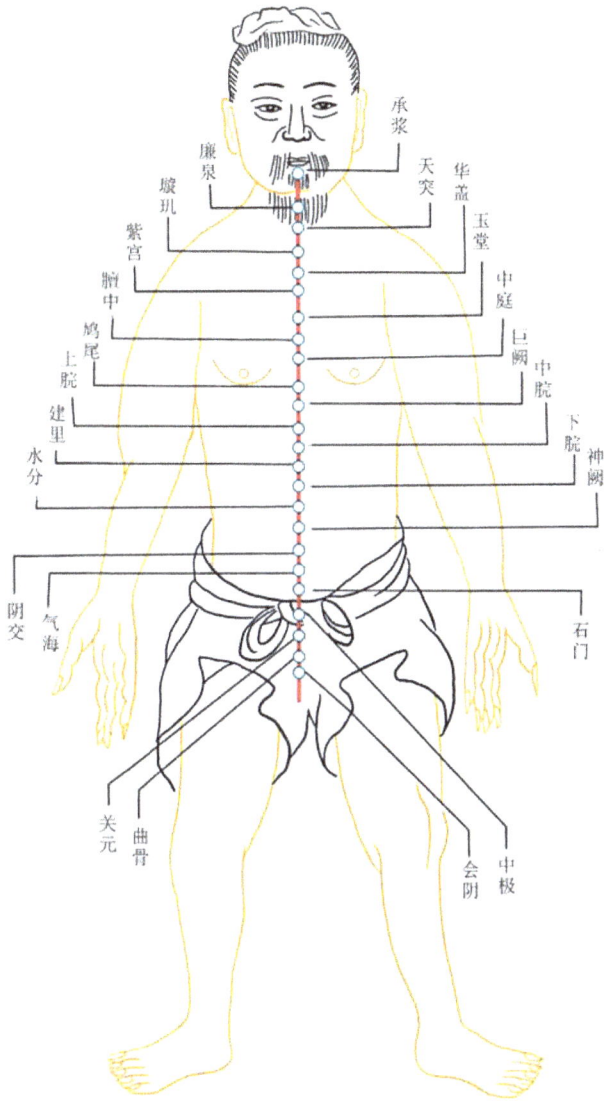

承浆
廉泉
璇玑
紫宫
膻中
鸠尾
上脘
建里
水分
阴交
气海
关元
曲骨

天突
华盖
玉堂
中庭
巨阙
中脘
下脘
神阙
石门
会阴
中极

# 任脉

Conception Vessel (Ren)

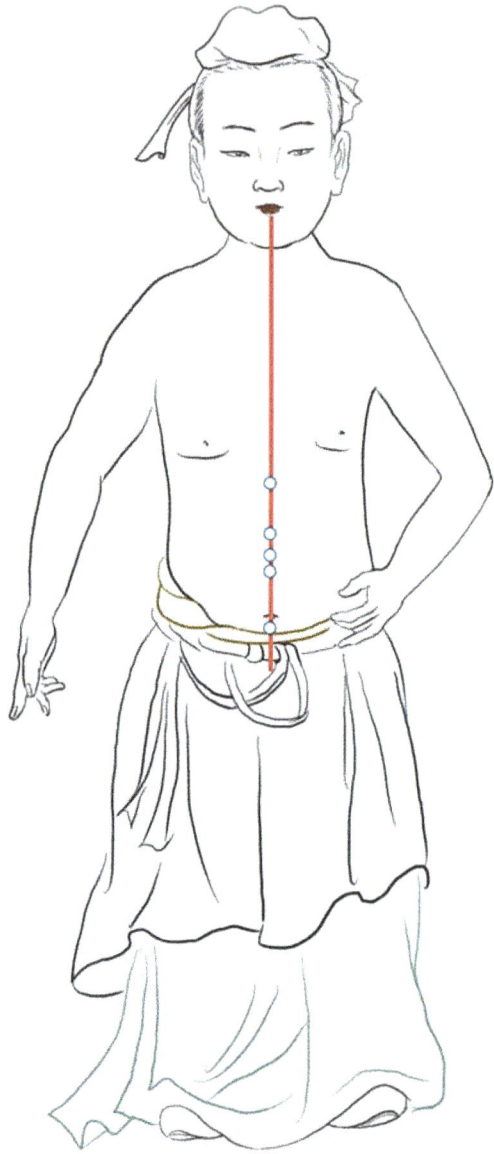

## 冲脉

Thoroughfare Vessel (Chong)

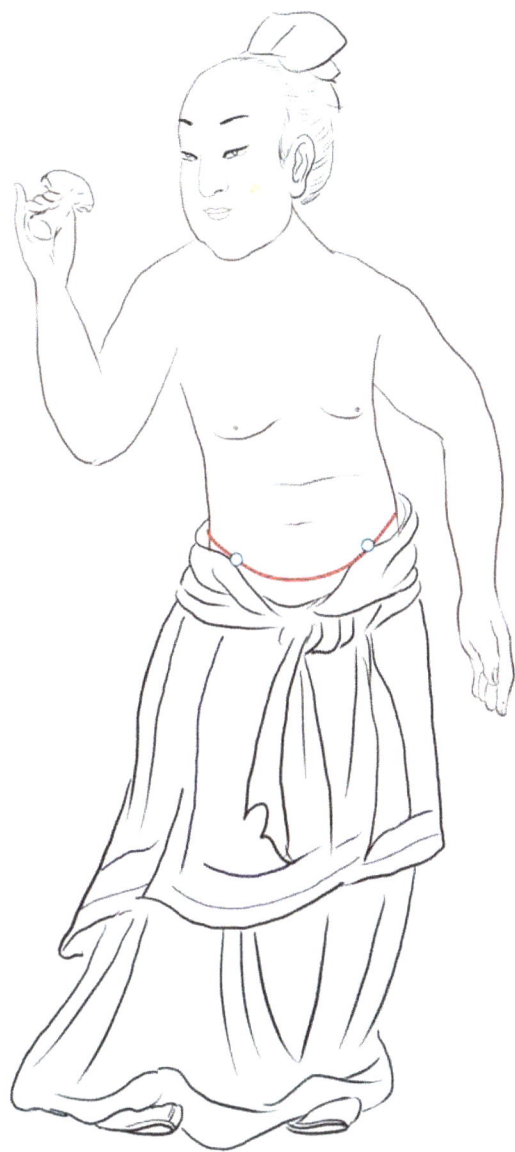

带脉

Belt Vessel (Dai)

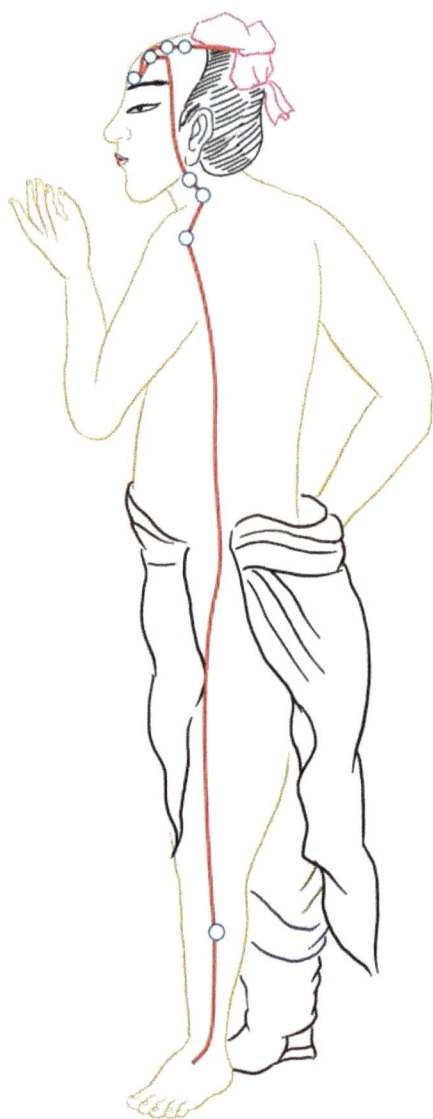

阳维脉

Yang Link Vessel (Yang Wei)

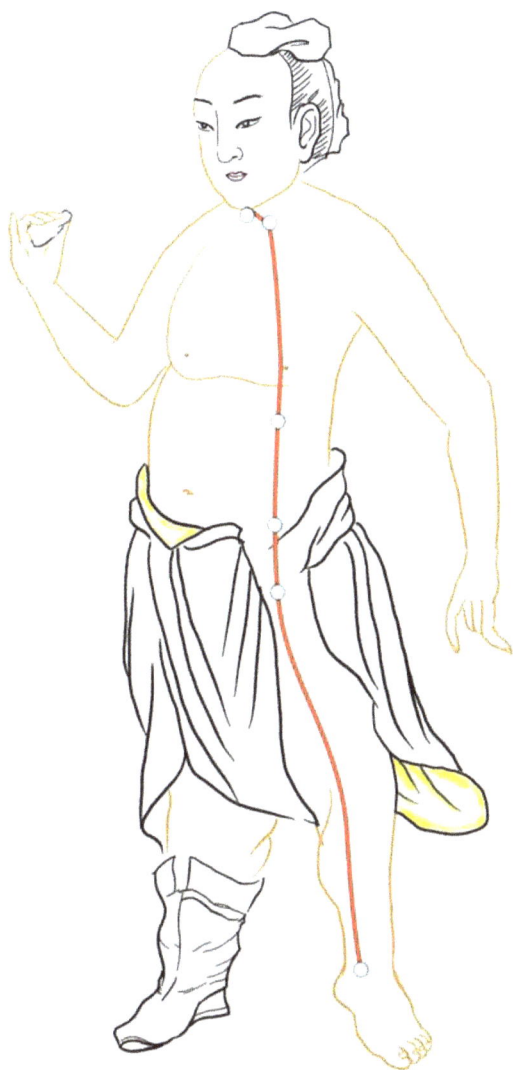

阴维脉

Yin Link Vessel (Yin Wei)

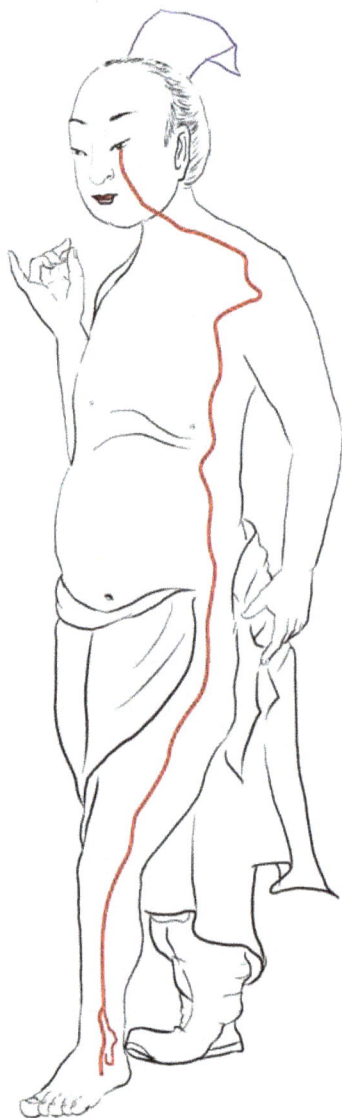

阳蹻脉

Yang Heel Vessel (Yang Qiao)

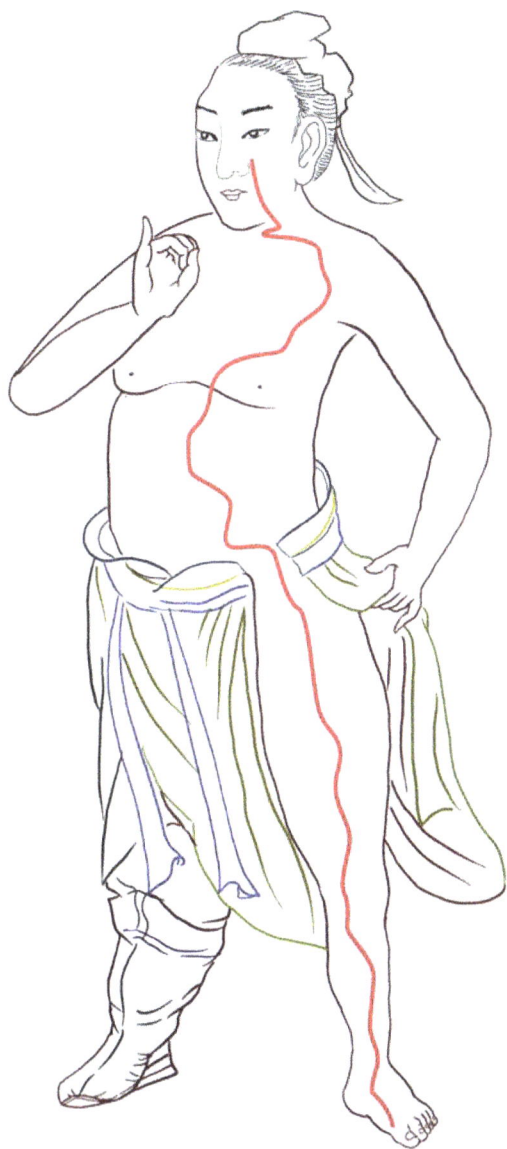

阴蹻脉

Yin Heel Vessel (Yin Qiao)

www.ingramcontent.com/pod-product-compliance
Lightning Source LLC
Chambersburg PA
CBHW081330090426
42737CB00017B/3075